I JUST WANT TO HANG OUT WITH YOU

I JUST WANT TO HANG OUT WITH YOU

JEN MANN

AND SOME LONELY MAMA BEARS

THROAT PUNCH MEDIA, LLC

CONTENTS

Introduction
By Jen Mann   ix

1. I HAD TO LET MY TEENS GO BEFORE I WAS   1
   READY
   By Katie Bingham-Smith
2. LEARNING TOGETHER   5
   By Susanne Kerns
3. SHOULD FEMINIST PARENTS TELL THEIR   9
   DAUGHTERS THEY ARE BEAUTIFUL?
   By Veronica I. Arreola
4. THE 100% ABSOLUTELY TRUE STORY OF HOW   13
   MY KID ACCIDENTALLY JOINED A CARTEL
   By Ava Mallory
5. THE ELECTION OF 1800   19
   By April Grant
6. 13 ESSENTIAL TRUTHS MY 13-YEAR-OLD   23
   TAUGHT ME ABOUT RAISING A TEEN GIRL
   By Galit Breen
7. THE JOY OF KNOWING MIDDLE SCHOOL   29
   DOESN'T MATTER
   By Erin Dymowski
8. LET'S TALK ABOUT SEX   35
   by Amy Rosenberg
9. MOOD SWINGS: I LEARNED IT BY WATCHING   41
   YOU
   By Cat Hollyer
10. READING IS FUNDAMENTAL (TO RAISING   47
    TEENAGERS)
    By Kim Bongiorno
11. RAISED WITH GRACE   53
    By Nicole Feltz
12. HIGHBROW TEENAGE ANGST   57
    By Holly Rutchik
13. OF HOODIES AND LEGENDS   63
    By K. Beck

14. I'M NOT LIKE A REGULAR MOM, I'M AN   71
UNCOOL MOM
By Heather Reed

15. A CAMEL, SOME STRAWS, AND YOUR   77
COLLEGE-BOUND TEEN
By Ellen Williams

16. PARENTAL WHIPLASH   85
By Suzanne Fleet

17. SCREEN TIME   91
By Candy Mickels Mejia

18. THE LETTING GO   97
By Gretchen Kelly

19. MOTHER'S DAY   103
By Andrea Contreras

20. A HARD "C"   109
By Sara Weber

21. T.G.I.F.   113
By Gila Pfeffer

22. UNTANGLED   119
By Santorina Davis

23. NERDMASTE: THE DIVINE AWKWARD IN ME   125
HONORS THE DIVINE AWKWARD IN YOU
By Nanea Hoffman

24. SHAKE WHAT YOUR MAMA GAVE YA!   129
By Rachel Sobel

25. THE LAST TIME   135
By Alexandra Rosas

26. THE KIDS ARE ALL RIGHT   141
By Jen Mann

Notes from the Editor   145
Other Books Available   147

INTRODUCTION

BY JEN MANN

Seven years ago I had a husband, two small children, a full-time career, a part-time career, and a to-do list the length of my arm. Back then I dreamed about taking a vacation by myself. I dreamed about the day when my children would be old enough to wipe their own bottoms or cook their own meals. I was fantasizing about empty hotel rooms and desolate beaches, but really I would have been thrilled with a bathroom all to myself. I had the idea to publish the book *I Just Want to Pee Alone* and it went on to be a *New York Times* bestseller and launched a whole line of successful books to follow.

For years my kids were a good source of material for me. Raising little kids was hard, lonely work and I created a community of like-minded, tired mamas. But after a while, I wrote about them less and less. A few months ago I was speaking at a library and someone asked me why I rarely write about my kids anymore. My answer was, "Because they're boring teenagers now." It's true! When I first started writing my kids were adorable and funny. We're seven years down the road and now I have two surly teenagers who communicate with me through TikTok videos and text messages laced with more emojis than words. For Christmas this year, my son Venmo'd me and I was just thrilled he thought to give me a gift. I called it a parenting win. I have two normal teenagers who think I am the most embarrassing mom on the planet. Meanwhile, half the moms I know are dancing on TikTok and the other half are making White Claw memes. All I do is drop the f-bomb like a comma and complain about pants. It could be so much worse!

I was so naive when my kids were small. I truly thought potty-training was the biggest challenge I'd ever face. *Hahahahahahahaha!!* No one told me that teenagers are about a thousand times harder! Now I understand what all those old ladies meant when they'd say, "Enjoy this time..." They knew! But they didn't tell us! They didn't tell us that our precious little pumpkins would grow up into adult-size toddlers. I swear, my son made better choices when he was 5 than he does at 15! I raised my daughter to be strong and sassy, but now that strong, sassy girl is always talking back to me! And don't even get me started on the fact that they never want to hang out with me.

Me: Want to watch a movie?
Teenager: No, thanks.
Me: Want to go to dinner?
Teenager: [Pause.] Where you going?
Me: Wherever you want!
Teenager: [Pause.] No, thanks.
Me: Want to go shopping?
Teenager: Can we shop for a dog?
Me: No.
Teenager: No, thanks.
Me: Want to talk?
Teenager: What about?
Me: Whatever you want!
Teenager: [Pause.] No, thanks.
Me: Want a hug?
Teenager: Oh, my God. Absolutely not!

The days are long, but the years are short. My time with my kids under my roof is quickly running out. I worry that I haven't prepared them for the real world, that they'll forget the lessons I taught them, that my connection with them isn't strong enough to survive the test of adulthood; but most of all, I worry they won't ever want to hang out with me again. At this point, every time I pee, I leave the bathroom door ajar, hoping for a visitor.

1

I HAD TO LET MY TEENS GO BEFORE I WAS READY

BY KATIE BINGHAM-SMITH

"Hi! What are you doing?" This is what my three teenagers hear from their rooms at least five times a day from the bottom of the stairs. It's my way of reminding them they have a mother who still wants a relationship with them, even if it means I have to strain my voice.

When my children were little, I didn't send them to daycare. I didn't want to. Not because I don't believe in it or think it's the wrong way to parent. It was my own selfish thoughts that kept them by my side day in and day out. I didn't want to be away from them any more than I had to be. Looking back, my mental health took a bit of a blow —I would have been a better mom had I taken my family and friends up on their offers to watch my kids—but it is what is it.

In the back of my mind, I knew this time would come—the days where shoulder shrugs have replaced the long, drawn-out stories with every detail of their day on repeat, the times when it took them forever to tell a story and they needed me to do everything for them despite their father standing right in front of them.

I knew Friday night pizza in front of kid-friendly shows would be something we used to do.

I knew they'd press the pause button on coming to me for advice.

I knew my daughter wanting to dress exactly like me would slowly morph into wanting to be the furthest thing from me.

What I didn't know was how bad it would rip me up. How much it would hurt and the angst it would cause. I thought I'd be more ready to see adult-looking versions of my kids share these four walls and not want a thing to do with me. And more than anything, I thought I was ready for this so-called "break." You know, the time in their lives where they are more self-sufficient and don't need their parents as much.

That's how it goes when they grow up and start to discover who they are as individuals. It's kind of like when someone you've been wanting to break up with does something bad—it's so much easier when you can blame the other person for the reason your relationship is ending.

I think about that every time my kids look at me and roll their eyes when I try to hug them at drop-off or ask if I can chaperone the dance. Apparently, that's grounds for dismissal in teenage-land. *How dare I?*

Everything is humiliating to my teens despite the fact that their friends think I'm cool—something I feel the need to remind them of at least twice a week.

In a sense, for the past three years, my teenagers have left me. One by one they've broken my heart. It comes in the form of not returning a hug. Not wanting to come Christmas shopping with me. Not listening to my warning, then doing some stupid.

I'm constantly surrounded by three humans who are taller than me and think they know much more than I do. I have three mouths to feed and put myself on hold constantly because being their mom is my number one job right now.

And I'm lonelier than I have ever been. Even lonelier than the years I lived alone in my 20s and did nothing but work and eat Hostess cupcakes for breakfast in my car each morning because I was hellbent on getting to work before anyone else.

I had a goal then; I was driven. My isolation was by choice. I knew all too well the power wine coolers and dance clubs had on me, so I stayed away. Furthering my career was all that mattered.

Now, my kids are all that matter to me, which is why I decided to let them go earlier than I was ready, to stop swimming against the tide and trying to turn back the clock.

The fact that they no longer want to spend much time with me is devastating. I miss who we used to be.

But mourning that made me feel so much worse.

I can't pull them back. I have to change with them lest I completely lose them, and myself, in the process. I need to reclaim some of the things that used to fulfill me before I became their mom.

Not working myself into the ground while living off cupcakes, mind you, but getting my life on track. Or this loneliness won't fade.

I never want my kids to feel responsible for my loneliness.

This in no way means I'm not supportive or am failing my kids.

It means I'm letting them do their thing (while I do more of mine) without the constant reminder that I liked our old life better. The life where they loved me and wanted to be with me and answered me in complete sentences.

I run. I go out with my friends more. I paint. I get massages and have started writing my first book. I go to spin class twice a week. I have let my kids see me "get a life" before they leave because it feels like the right thing to do. For me and for them.

Besides, I've heard they come back around. I'm willing to wait but I might as well do me in the meantime.

KATIE BINGHAM-SMITH HAD three kids in three years and crafts her ass off in order to stay sane. She loves to write, wear faux leather pants, eat at burger joints, and make beautiful things. She pays her kids to rub her feet and play with her hair. You can follow @katiebinghamsmith to see more of her work on Facebook and Instagram.

LEARNING TOGETHER

BY SUSANNE KERNS

I still remember it like it was yesterday.

My 14-year-old daughter and I sat quietly, knees to knees, staring deep into each other's eyes. I held my breath as she struggled to find the words she was searching for, forcing myself to resist my natural mothering instinct to jump in and save her.

Let her struggle so she can learn.

Let her feel the pride of transforming discomfort into words.

Let her grow.

Finally, when I was just about to give in to my impulse and suggest my own words in place of those she could not say, she took a deep breath and said:

"My uncle's table is big, heavy, and purple."

I smiled, full of pride, and replied, "My neighbor's table is flat, long, and orange."

We both exhaled a sigh of relief and giggled at our infant-level sign language skills.

It was our final week of sign language class, and after spending every Thursday night of the summer together, we had finally leveled up to stringing nouns, verbs, and adjectives together to make actual (although maybe not useful with people who aren't super into tables) sentences.

I wish I could take credit for coming up with the idea of registering us for sign language classes to spend more time together, but it was all my daughter's idea. This is the same girl that spent her entire sixth grade winter break trying to learn Portuguese so the new classmate from Brazil would have someone to talk to at lunch. When I asked her why she wanted to learn sign language, she answered in a traditional 14-year-old "*duh*, Mom" tone: "So if I ever meet someone who can't hear, I can still talk to them."

(Side note: In case you are like me and wondering if teenagers can still have a "*duh*, Mom" tone in sign language, our teacher's kids attended one of our classes once, and rest assured, teenagers are very capable of giving epic eye rolls and head shakes even when their hands are occupied.)

I hesitate to suggest registering for sign language classes just to spend time with your teen because that is completely ableist and feels like turning someone's physical challenge into a hobby. However, if your heart and intentions are like my daughter's—truly wanting to open up the world of communication with those who use sign language—you may find that taking an ASL class together has the added benefit of opening up a world of conversations between you and your teen.

It's not the first time sign language has helped us communicate. When she was an infant, baby sign language was a magical gift, transforming generic "I'm pissed off" baby screams into, "I want milk," "More sweet potatoes, please," or "MORE GERBER PUFFS, RIGHT DAMN NOW!"

Back then, I was the teacher. Now, in an ASL classroom, I am very much the student. So much so that when the real teacher asked us all to introduce ourselves on the first day of class, my daughter had to step in and introduce me, "Her name is S-U-S-A-N-N-E." The only signs I could offer were an embarrassed shrug and wave. I almost broke the main no-voices classroom rule to ask, "How the hell did you know how to say that?" but instead used the one sign I remembered from the baby signs book to simply say, "Thank you."

There is something truly wonderful about the power dynamic shift of having your child come to your rescue. But even if your teen hasn't been secretly practicing sign language through online tutorials for months so they're able to save your ass in an Intro to ASL class, just being on a level playing field and learning something together is a wonderful break from always being the person who pretends to have all the answers.

The most unexpected connection we formed from the class came from the sensory deprivation experience of not being able to speak during the class. Despite being in class together for three months, we knew almost nothing about the other sixteen people in our class. Due to our lack of sign vocabulary, we only knew each other's names and occasionally, if it related to a lesson, their favorite food or what clothing they would pack for a vacation. I guess we could have cheated in the bathrooms or in the halls after class, but we honored the code of silence and instead struggled to make small talk through what turned out to be a game of signing telephone. I would mistakenly say, "I have a son. He is 200 years old and very furry," but it wouldn't matter because they would hear, "I stole twenty cars from that squirrel."

You may think that your teen doesn't have much to say to you, but after two hours of speech and text deprivation, they will talk about absolutely anything you want during the entire car ride home just to exercise the privilege of voice and being understood.

The same sense of empathy that drove my daughter to want to learn how to sign in the first place was magnified by the experience of silence. On the drives home from class, when our pent-up words burst out as soon as we closed the car doors, she would ask, "How would we talk while you're driving if we were deaf and couldn't sign?" Or one day while we were kneading bread, she asked, fingers all webbed together with dough, "How would I ask you to hand me the flour?" I assured her that just like we don't have to enunciate perfectly and speak the Queen's English to be understood, those who depend on sign have also developed workarounds to communicate in less than ideal situations. Discussing these questions has helped us appreciate that it's a privilege to have so many options of how and with whom we communicate. And we realize how often we take it for granted.

Despite the profound insights into the variety of options for human dialogue we gained during our summer of ASL, we have let our signing practice slide and instead primarily converse by me shouting, "DINNER!" up the stairs or her texting, "Can you bring me up some goldfish crackers?" But a few months ago, she came home from school and told me that she spoke sign language to two strangers who were signing on the bus. I barely have the courage to make eye contact with people on the bus, but she got their attention and said, "Hello. I'm learning sign language. It is sunny today."

Just like that first day of class when she had to introduce me, I was in awe of her courage and her desire to connect and communicate with everyone regardless of language. This summer we're practicing French and taking ASL 201 together, because, as she says, you never know when you're going to meet someone you want to talk to. And as I say, you never turn down your teenage daughter when she wants to talk to you.

SUSANNE KERNS IS a humor writer living in Austin, Texas with her husband and two children. Her work has been featured in *Scary Mommy, Redbook, Today Parents* and several parenting anthologies. She's currently writing her first non-fiction book. and also runs "Informed Parents of Austin," a group she founded to advocate for LGBTQIA+ students, families, and staff in her school district. She spends an unhealthy amount of time on Facebook, but you can also find her on Instagram at @susannekerns, where she posts her tasteful nudes.* (*photos of poorly lit food, and animals, all nude), or on Twitter whenever she accidentally opens the wrong app on her phone.

SHOULD FEMINIST PARENTS TELL THEIR DAUGHTERS THEY ARE BEAUTIFUL?

BY VERONICA I. ARREOLA

O r perhaps I should ask HOW should feminist parents tell their daughters they are beautiful?

In 2015 I attended Tamara Winfrey Harris's book reading at Women and Children First, a bookstore in Chicago. She read from her book, *The Sisters Are Alright: Changing the Broken Narrative of Black Women in America*, which discusses how Black women are viewed in the USA and their reactions to those views. One area of discussion was that of beauty.

In 2014 I launched a hashtag challenge, #365FeministSelfie, in response to media reports that selfies could only be harmful. I challenged friends and social media followers to seek out the feminist angle, to toss out the social messages that tell us to look for our flaws, and instead spend one moment a day looking at ourselves and learning to, maybe, love what we saw.

As #365FeministSelfie went viral, people used the space to grapple and discuss many issues. At its core is the concept of beauty: *Who gets to say who is beautiful? Why don't more women believe they are beautiful?* During the life of the project, I have heard from many people, especially women, who confess to never feeling beautiful or losing that sense of beauty.

A mom in the project shared a moment from her mom files.

She shared that her 3-year-old daughter had just pronounced herself "not-beautiful" because of her short hair. I'm paraphrasing here: "Help me, #365FeministSelfie-ists! How can I combat this? I tell her she's strong, smart, and brave all the time, but I don't always tell her she is beautiful." A few of us went on to discuss the often-held notion that it's better to praise girls for what they do, not how they look. You have probably seen the memes offering guidance on how to talk to young girls without praising their beauty or clothes: *Ask them about books they are reading, what they are learning in school, basically anything that is not about their looks.* This should allow them to escape the clutches of our beauty-centric society, right? Wrong.

Unless we are raising our daughters in a media-free bubble in the middle of Big Sky Country, they still learn the rules of beauty. They still learn that long hair is more beautiful than short. That thinner is better. Girls as young as elementary school know what a thigh gap is and want to have one.

In 2019, Weight Watchers launched an app for children as young as 8 to use.

The backlash was loud, and the company who taught our mothers to hate themselves responded with data about childhood obesity. How do we fight this battle when even government data is trying to teach us to hate ourselves?

At the reading, I asked Tamara and her fans how to handle this. I was floored by their responses.

One woman, whose story is shared in the book, said that when she was growing up, all she wanted was her mom to say she was beautiful. Her mom, like many feminist-minded moms, was trying to raise a strong girl who did not need that type of validation. Now, this woman did not fit the beauty standard as a young girl and teen, so her mom was trying to get her to see her own beauty inside and out. "Do you think you are beautiful?" was what her mom would say when asked, "Am I beautiful/pretty?" This woman proclaimed to us, "All I wanted was for my mom to say, 'Yes, you are beautiful!'"

Since then I tell my daughter that she is beautiful all the time.

The fact of the matter is that a lot of people tell her that too. When she meets people for the first time, people look at me and exclaim, "She's so beautiful!" It is always awkward and weird. Do I say, "Thank you?" as if I am taking credit?

I settled on telling her she is beautiful often in a series of other compliments. "You are so strong, smart, beautiful, and brave, mija!" My daughter is a great soccer player, a loving friend, and does great in school. I want her to embrace all those things.

It's strange, this beauty thing. On the one hand, we do not want to raise our daughters to think their beauty, or whether others see them as beautiful, defines them. But at the same time, don't we all want to feel beautiful?

And that is what #365FeministSelfie is about—feeling beautiful in our bodies, feeling as beautiful as those who love us see us. Rejecting the social messages that say beauty is only for the thin, the young, and/or "appropriately sized" bodies. Seeing our flaws as our beauty. Rejecting the framing of flaws! Embracing that overweight bodies are healthy bodies. Because yes, beauty is in the eyes of the beholder, but it should be in our eyes too.

So, does withholding praise of our daughters' beauty tell them they are not beautiful? And this despite the fact that we are trying to teach them that being beautiful is not important? What do they learn when we say nothing at all?

Studies have shown that girls learn to hate their bodies earlier if their parents, especially their mothers, are vocal with their own body hate. This fact has been one of my biggest guiding points as a parent. No matter how much I struggle with my body image or health issues, I try to hold those negative thoughts to myself or share them with close friends. But should I have been sharing all the times when I thought I looked great that day? When my hair behaved, make-up looked fabulous, outfit came together, and I walked out the door on cloud nine? What messages could I have sent by embracing my own beauty?

In the end Tamara made a pronouncement that I think is correct: *Everyone should be told they are beautiful*. Perhaps we should all compliment our kids and each other with, "You are so beautiful, smart, strong, and brave."

VERONICA I. ARREOLA is a professional feminist, writer, and soccer mom. Her writing has been featured in *USA Today*, *The New York Times*, as well as Bitch Media, where Veronica serves on the board of directors. Veronica's pandemic project was to jump into the podcast pool with *The Feminist Agenda*, where she talks to other professional feminists about their work and how they stay organized. By day she works on diversity in science issues at the University of Illinois at Chicago. Veronica is the founder of the 50th Ward Action Network, a collective of politically minded neighbors on the far northside of Chicago where she lives with her husband and their high-school-aged daughter. You can follow @veronicaeye on Twitter and Instagram.

THE 100% ABSOLUTELY TRUE STORY OF HOW MY KID ACCIDENTALLY JOINED A CARTEL

BY AVA MALLORY

B oys are born with no common sense and I can prove it. Pardon me as I channel my inner Sophia Petrillo. Picture this. The year was 2019. The skies were blueish. The sun had just come up. The mom (me) was mumbling something not fit for daytime TV under her breath as she cleaned up the remains of a Sunday evening homemade pizza massacre that destroyed Calorie Central, the kitchen, and the Landing Pad Room, the dining room where every conceivable and nearly inconceivable item that comes into the house lands, never to be seen or heard from again. The villagers (read: teenage children) were in their usual habitat—their respective bedrooms on cellphones seconds after the mom threatened to purge everything they own if they didn't hurry and get dressed for school.

After twenty minutes the mom and teenage children couldn't spare, they finally emerged from their hastily cleaned habitat and ventured out into the wild, the dreaded school drop-off line, where the mom routinely entered glaring contests with other harried parents just as eager to drop off their complaining teenagers. As the family neared the Promised Land, the designated drop-off point, her phone went abuzz.

"Who is texting me at 7 a.m.?" She muttered through gritted teeth.

"I'll check," the teenage boy who never volunteers for anything volunteered as he singlehandedly unlatched the mom's purse, reached in, found a pack of gum that he quickly pocketed, and removed the phone from its designated pocket—the one the mom could never find when it rang in public. "It's for me."

Careful to keep her eyes on the cars in front of her in case the police officer who directed school traffic was watching, the mom said through a fake smile, "Why is someone texting you on *my* phone?"

There used to be a time when the male child's laugh could make the mom's heart sing, but this was not the time, and her heart's ability to sing died when said child first destroyed something that belonged to her years earlier.

The mom inched the car forward, mere yards from the Promised Land.

"Explain."

"It's nothing," the teenage boy said as he dutifully placed the phone back in the purse. "Just if you see a package at the house, and it has a weird name on it, it's for me."

They'd finally reached the Promised Land and the mom couldn't have been more elated. In fact, she was so excited to purge her vehicle of the teenagers, she completely forgot to interrogate the male child about the package. Instead, she practically shoved the kids out of her car and talked herself out of peeling off like a getaway driver in front of the police officer.

"Have a good day! Do good things!" she called out as she waited for the officer to give her the go-ahead to leave.

It wasn't until she sprinted for the front door that she remembered the mystery box. There it was on the front porch. It was the size of a mini-fridge and weighed about as much. The mom would've carried the box inside had she had her Wheaties prior to rushing her kids to school, but alas, she had not. That's when she noticed the name on the mailing label: Dick Johnson.

Now that's a fine name if that happens to be your name, but the teenage boy had mentioned something about the box being for him. Clearly, it wasn't.

In an unwise attempt to give the kid the benefit of the doubt, the mom did as the child asked and took the box inside for safekeeping, foolishly believing she'd remember to interrogate the child later. As expected, the mom forgot, and the male teenager took advantage of the mom's forgetfulness and kept the box out of her sight.

Exactly one week later, another mysterious box arrived on their doorstep. This time it was addressed to Suzy Q. Sunshine.

Thankfully, the mom had had her coffee that morning and had the wherewithal to scream for the male teenager at the top of her lungs.

"What now?" he called out, exasperated.

"What's the deal with these boxes?"

The silence that followed was the first sign the boy was up to no good.

"I know you heard me."

He descended the stairs, chin on chest. "I heard you."

"Why do we keep getting boxes with other people's names on them?" It seemed like a logical question.

His response, however, wasn't anything close to logical.

"I wanted to surprise you." He waited a beat, then said, "Surprise!"

The mom was sure she was human, but the sound that came out of her mouth was anything but human.

"Mom," he pleaded. "I'll take care of it."

This is when the teenage girl emerged from her lair. "I told you it was a dumb idea."

"Shut up!"

"Don't tell your sister to shut up!"

"Can we do this later? We're going to be late for class," the boy said.

Mom was so taken aback by his sudden desire to get to school on time, she tabled the conversation because surely the boy hadn't done anything wrong.

Boy, was the mom wrong!

She dutifully took her eager children to school and drove home with a smile on her face and her superwoman pajamas on her body.

Those pajamas would come back to haunt her shortly.

"Ma'am?" A police officer about half her age stood at the front door. "Are you…"

He knew her name!

She gulped. "Yes, is something wrong?"

He smiled. "Not necessarily. Do you have a minute to talk?" His gaze fell to her pajamas.

Feeling exposed, the mom used her trembling hands as shields. "Is everything okay?" She glanced at her car. "Did I take a stop sign?"

He shook his head, the smile still on his face. "No, nothing like that. I'm actually here to talk to you about your son."

The mom's heart lodged in her throat. She couldn't breathe. Her feet would no longer hold her.

The officer grabbed her arm to steady her. "It's okay, ma'am. I just want to talk to you about the mail."

"The mail?"

"A couple of boxes that were delivered to your house."

Her life flashed before her eyes. Her son's life flashed before her eyes.

This was it. Life as she knew it was over.

"Do you want to go inside?" he asked.

"No, give me the bad news here."

He glanced at her pajamas again. "I think maybe we should get you inside."

It took several agonizing seconds before she pulled herself together and opened the door to let the officer in.

He stood in the doorway. "It's come to our attention that your son has been in communication with a company based out of Miami."

"A company? What company?"

"Has he told you about his job?"

"Job? What job? He's 15. He doesn't work."

The officer scratched his head. "Did he receive a couple of boxes in the mail?"

"Yes, but they weren't for him."

"Where are they?" he asked.

She had no idea.

"Ma'am?" The officer pulled a notebook out of his pocket. "Let me show you something." He showed her the name and address of a company. "Have you ever heard of this business?"

"No."

He sighed. "Do you have the boxes?"

"Yes?"

"Yes, you know that for sure?"

She shrugged because what did she know?

"Is my son in trouble?"

He shook his head. "Not unless he knew what he got involved in."

"What did he get involved in?"

The officer went on to explain that the boxes were part of a theft ring that funds cartel activity. The fake company dupes innocent people into receiving boxes to inspect then send to a particular post office box. They "hire" people under the guise of a legitimate work-at-home job, but that's not what it is. They steal credit card numbers and test the waters by buying small items, then, trick someone like the teenage boy into shipping them for them. Eventually, the small items would contain "product" for the cartel or would involve items of increasing value that they bought with someone else's credit card.

"Oh my God!" She nearly fainted. "My kid is in the cartel? How did you find out?"

He explained that they'd been working with the FBI since they became aware that some local folks were duped into accepting a job with them.

What in the actual...?

And that's how her son accidentally joined the cartel!

From that day until about the time the child marries, the teenage male spends his days and nights and weekends and holidays doing everything his mother tells him without complaint, because although the mom can be quite forgetful, she'll never forget the day the police showed up at her door to inform her that the FBI had been alerted to his possible involvement with a theft ring run by a MOTHER TRUCKING CARTEL.

AVA MALLORY HAS BEEN a grade schoolteacher, a psychiatric technician, a dementia unit nurse manager, a hospice nurse, and now a *USA Today* and *Wall Street Journal* bestselling author. She has embarrassed herself in front of handsome celebrities, won vocal contests much to the chagrin of her children, survived a major earthquake, and nearly drowned when she mistakenly thought a YMCA lifeguard asked her to dive into the deep end on her first day of swim lessons. She and her eternally annoyed children share their home with a massive collection of books and a never-ending supply of new book ideas.

AVA IS BEST KNOWN for what she calls her "Mysteries with Heart." She loves a great madcap adventure with lovable, yet ornery and sometimes precocious characters who play hard, laugh often, never mind their own business, bicker, squabble, and tease relentlessly, but never forget that deep down they fiercely love each other, even if they can't bring themselves to admit it. Follow @avascozymysterieswithheart on Facebook.

THE ELECTION OF 1800

BY APRIL GRANT

Coming home after a long day, I started my nighttime routine of disrobing, making myself a night cap, and checking my phone for the final time for the evening.

Normally, there's nothing to note or even see when I do this final check. My friends know that I turn off my phone early. To say I was surprised would be an understatement when I received this message at 8:01 p.m.: "I just got two tickets to *Hamilton*, if you are out and about."

See, this day wasn't just any day; it was my son's sixteenth birthday and he's a huge *Hamilton* fan. He had purchased the soundtrack two years prior and knew every song by heart, even though he hadn't seen a lick of the show. In an attempt to get tickets for him, I entered the *Hamilton* daily drawing to win free tickets and the final day was just two days away. The cheapest tickets I saw were $300 for the pair and that was not in our budget. I even put out a request on Facebook to my friends and family to see if they had any to "spare," as if that was even a possibility.

Immediately, I responded "What? You mean in your hands? For when? Yes! Jeff's out and about!" I didn't hesitate to put my clothes back on even though I was unsure about what was going on. I was excited, confused, anxious, and ready to go pick up the tickets.

My confusion only intensified after the next text from my friend: "No for tonight and it's just starting...the lady left them under a trashcan for me..."

What the what?

I couldn't really comprehend what she was saying but as it was already after the show's starting time of 8 p.m., I decided to figure it out later—well, in the car. So between getting dressed again and calling for my son to do the same, I texted her for clarification.

The tickets were under a trash can INSIDE the venue. Apparently, the original ticket holder couldn't offload them to anyone and at the last minute was contacted by my friend. Since she was already at the theater, ready for the show, she just left them under the trashcan right outside the door to the theater.

Thankfully, the theater was only ten minutes away driving normally, but that night I had a lead foot, so I made it there in about seven. But I had only been to this venue once before, and this situation was strange to say the least.

We ran up to the window and as I explained the situation, the will call attendant replied, "No problem, just go inside." Again, this night was full of confusion.

"I can go inside?"

"Sure," she responded. "You only need a ticket to take a seat, not to enter the building."

My anxiety started to subside as excitement moved in. We quickly went to the front door and explained the situation (again). As kind as they could be, the manager responded, "Would you like one of our ushers to help you look?"

I wasn't even sure where I was going and anything that would expedite getting us into our seats was beyond helpful. Even the usher moved quickly and took us directly to the black trashcan outside of section 3U. Sure enough, there were two tickets for that night's show right there.

A second usher welcomed us in. We were able to catch our breath while we stood in the aisle waiting to be seated.

When we finally did sit down, we found out who our gracious ticket purchasers were, and they would not shut up. They kept asking, "Are you the ones we sold the tickets to?" and "Are you supposed to be here?" I kept responding while nodding, "Yes, I will tell you at intermission."

Finally, we had the opportunity to see *Hamilton*—in quiet.

At intermission, I got clarification of everything that had happened that led me to be able to catch 90% of *Hamilton* live.

Our seat neighbors were price shopping on the website, opening tabs for different days and times. Apparently, when she pressed purchase, she had already chosen two seats in another tab, plus the two seats in this tab, thus purchasing four tickets. After repeated unsuccessful attempts to get a refund, she posted on the general *Hamilton* Facebook page that she had two tickets for sale. No one commented but my friend.

My friend had full intentions of attending *Hamilton* with her husband and two sons. Hubs and one son had successfully found two tickets in the same row across the theater. However, her younger son wasn't having it and didn't want to go. She couldn't leave him alone and her first thought was to reach out to me, knowing I wanted to take my son.

I Cashapp'd my new seat buddy payment for the tickets and made our way down to the lobby to grab some merch. We are a frugal family and I have taught my son not to put too much value in "stuff." So, when he looked at the options, his eyes went straight to the *Hamilton* hoodie. As a teenage boy, hoodies are staples of his wardrobe.

He hesitated to ask me after seeing the $70 price tag. He knows I'm more comfortable spending the same amount at Goodwill and buying a dozen items than spending that amount on one large-ticket item. But I also know anything I purchase for him will be used until it can't be used any more, and therefore I was happy to get it for him.

Immediately, you could see how happy he was, cheesing from ear to ear. He promptly put it on and wore it as we returned to our seats.

During the second half of the show, you could clearly see he was getting tired. He's a good sleeper and is normally knocked out by 10 p.m., but this was a three-hour show, so he had another hour to go. He laid his head on my shoulder but quickly popped it up so he didn't fall asleep.

After getting back into the car, we relaxed and chatted while waiting for the traffic to clear. My son laid back, fell asleep, and I knew he enjoyed his gift for his sixteenth birthday.

APRIL NOELLE GRANT is the founder of *The Other Side of 40*, is an experienced entrepreneur with a passion for helping women. She started her career as a lawyer but changed paths so she could be in a more supportive role to her family. She started the blog *April Noelle* in 2011 to help mothers by offering tips and tricks. She recently pivoted her company to include implementing systems and supporting growth for women-owned small businesses. Her heart beats with the love of her long-time husband and four children. Follow @otherside40 on Instagram.

6

13 ESSENTIAL TRUTHS MY 13-YEAR-OLD TAUGHT ME ABOUT RAISING A TEEN GIRL

BY GALIT BREEN

1**. Her personality has arrived.**

My newly minted teenager has a more defined silliness and sarcasm, sense of style, and stronger opinions about her clothes, activities, and the way she spends her time. Some of this is negotiable and some of it isn't—I expect her to be present for family activities, and I don't have a problem vetoing weather-inappropriate clothing, but I respect her need to figure out how she presents herself to the world—even (especially?) if it's different than I would have imagined.

2. She's sweet.

And kind. And empathetic. I know that teenagers have a bad reputation. And yes, there's moodiness in our house sometimes, but that's true of all of us, isn't it? I think, in the deepest crevices of my mama heart, what I'm really feeling when I cry, "Teen surliness!" is the shift from little to big, mine to independent. When I've been able to loosen my grip on her smallness, I've been privy to an amazing human being right in front of my eyes. There's an unparalleled kindness and empathy to this age group. I absolutely want to nurture that, and then get out of her way so that she can maneuver this world of ours in what I absolutely believe can be a teen trademark—radical kindness.

3. Faith in her is key.

There's a place for worrying and, goodness knows, I'm good at it. But in my heart of hearts, I know that worrying sends my daughter the subtle message that I don't think she can do "this," whatever "this" may be in any given moment. And I'd so much rather (loudly) suggest that I believe in her. And if the absolute worst thing that can happen happens, and she falls, I'll be there to cheer her on as she pulls herself right back up.

4. She's still learning.

My teen is going to make mistakes. And if my time as a teenager —and let's face it, as an adult—is any indication, she's going to make lots of them! I know that it's my job to help her learn from those mistakes, fix them, and do more good in this world than harm.

5. She still needs me.

I'm awestruck by my teen's independence daily, and it's so easy to think, *She's got this.* But when we're home at the same time, I do my best to make myself available to her. I might just be doling out snacks when she gets home or sitting on the couch while she does homework or out back while she's "hanging out," but I'm there. And every single day, at some random, often inconvenient time, she tells or asks or shares something I would have missed if I had chosen to be someplace else.

6. I'll never regret advocating for her.

I believe this with every fiber of my being. I have not once regretted advocating for my teen or helping her form the words to advocate for herself. But I do regret the times when, for a variety of truly unimportant reasons, I didn't do this. Even if—when!—I've spoken too soon or too loud or when I've needed to backtrack later... honestly, who cares? I'm laser-focused on making her feel less alone as she maneuvers this world.

7. She's sensitive.

That newfound sarcasm can make my girl's heart seem tough at times, but I know it's not. With growth and change comes vulnerability and nothing describes what this age group is going through better than growth and change! So when I've been lucky enough to have her let me into that vulnerability alongside her—in on her worries and her thoughts and her opinions; into her heart, really—I've learned to thank my lucky stars for that moment, and to spend more time listening to her heart than trying to change it, lest she stop sharing it with me.

8. She craves my approval.

This is a tough one for me to remember especially as my girl is growing and learning and doing so very much, so very fast. But every once in a while, maybe when she's shared or tried or done something new, I catch this look in her eyes. And even though those eyes are now set above newly slender and blushed and oh-so-very-grown up cheeks, the look I've caught a glimpse of is identical to the one she used to give me when she was teeny-tiny and she'd look up at me, wide-eyed and pudgy-cheeked, waiting to hear that I saw her, heard her, loved her. Those eyes are my pause and reminder to give her my approval freely, just like I did when she was little and more obviously in need of it.

9. I'm creating her framework for intimacy.

How I treat people and how I let people treat me is what my teen will know as normal. I know this includes how I talk to and about her, myself, and others. That's a hard pill to swallow! I'm trying so very hard to be so very mindful and so very intentional about that, because my instincts in this area are still a work in progress, and I want better for her.

10. She gets and knows and is exposed to so much more than I'd ever guess.

I've learned to ask for her thoughts before I tell her mine. And more often than not, she's already heard of the topic, researched it, and formed a strong opinion about it. I'm in awe of her mind and of her heart and how she twines the two to work together; I tell her so often and freely. This also means that I've learned to never water down our conversations. I share with her happy things and hard things and important things. And she's so here for these conversations; it's my job to meet her here.

11. In that same vein, I don't shy away from hard conversations.

Don't get me wrong, I definitely stumble, but then I dive right in there. Periods, love, sex, sexuality, depression, alcohol, drugs, kindness, bullying, friendship—I know it's a privilege to be my teen's soft landing, as well as the hard-message sender. I'm going to do my absolute best, as often as humanly possible, to not take myself so seriously as I stumble through, and act like I know that these hard conversations with her are 100% stumble-worthy, as is she. I want to model a good debate, a strong reaction, smart questions, and kind (re)actions. I'll keep practicing all of the above until she and I get it right-ish, together.

12. She's watching me for clues on how to maneuver this world as a woman.

I believe that strong, smart, and empathetic women are golden. What these adjectives have meant to me or how they've shown up for me throughout my life doesn't actually matter; it'll look different for her. But I still try to model for her, every day, what these mean to me when I follow my passions, speak my mind, and see my own value.

13. I'm her biggest fan.

I try to tell my teenager directly and often what a light she is in my life without worrying about spoiling her. I believe that compliments should be given daily and freely and with wild abandon and I can't think of a better place for me to practice this than with my teen. When I was in my teacher education program, my professor would regularly say that everyone deserves at least one person in their life who thinks they hung the moon. I want to fill my daughter's heart with shared moments and words and presence—with moonlight—until it's abundantly clear that I'm that person for her.

This list is more gender universal than not. But, for right now, I only know teen girls, so that's where my focus is.

∾

GALIT BREEN IS the bestselling author of *Kindness Wins,* a simple guide to teaching your child to be kind online and the TEDx Talk, "Raising a Digital Kid Without Having Been One." Galit is the co-director of the *Listen to Your Mother* show in the Twin Cities and her writing has been featured on *Huffington Post; The Washington Post; Buzzfeed; TIME*; and more. She lives in Minnesota with her husband, three children, and ridiculously spoiled mini goldendoodle.

7

THE JOY OF KNOWING MIDDLE SCHOOL DOESN'T MATTER

BY ERIN DYMOWSKI

During our time in coronavirus lockdown, in addition to basically transforming into a needy houseplant with substantial caloric needs, I read a lot. In particular, I remember reading a special edition of *The New York Times* that charmed me. The section was titled simply, "The Joy of . . ." Various authors tripped over themselves to refocus the reader's attention on the simple virtues of everything from a wonky old Nintendo to the "hate watch" to even just circling the block. What a gift in what could be referred to as not just a suckalicious time, but THE suckalicious time to rule all the times! I was going to steal this party trick and regift it to people in that other hellish landscape I inhabited, the one we call middle school.

Middle school, in many ways, does live up to its bad reputation. As a middle school teacher by profession, I'm a frontline survivor, and I can attest that it ain't pretty. The potent brew of hormones and low-level hostility percolating under all things prepubescent keeps emotions turned all the way up all the time. Even seemingly mundane interactions and old familiar routines cannot retain their formerly harmless veneer. All is washed in drama. All is drenched in innuendo. All is cloaked in bravado. And then everywhere, underneath it all, is fear—of being left out, left behind, left of center. When we call it hellish, we are dialing it back a bit.

As middle school is by design the on-ramp to all things teen, there's also a sense of the danger around the corner, and you can almost feel the rush of the coming years. In many ways, it feels potent and heavy. Add to this emotional pressure cooker the new academic stakes and parents can easily be forgiven for getting it all wrong, for investing heavily in what success looks like, rather than what it truly is at this stage. I'm going to insert here an example to illustrate my point, a typical email in the life of a middle school teacher:

Dear Mrs. Dymowski,

You are an educator who doesn't just hate my child but all children. You are an affront to education itself. Please excuse Petunia from her 10-point assignment. She had soccer, wreath-making class, and an appointment with her spiritual guru last night, all of which we deemed more important than your assignment.

Signed,
Someone Who ACTUALLY cares about kids

Now, I like my job and children, so I cannot offer all my legitimate but ultimately unhelpful responses, but I can offer some corrections.

Dear Misguided But Well-Meaning Parent,

Thank you for reaching out. Middle school today is harder than ever. Students are not just expected to read, but read to perform. They are not just expected to perform, but perform at the next level. In the race toward rigor, students who make it through the middle school front doors are literally gobsmacked with Bloom's Taxonomy of questions. The old familiar constructs of education which they have practiced for the past six years—

knowledge, comprehension, and application—are no longer the goals of an academic block.

In addition, the academic stakes are kicked up a notch just as kids' emotional bandwidth is taxed to the max. Yikes! I understand completely the value of that guru. This coupled with a new schedule that takes kids from a one teacher/one classroom model to the many teacher/multiple classroom model pushes all the kids' buttons. Kids at this point do what any non-rational, hormonal being would do: stop functioning, shut down completely, turn themselves off literally and figuratively. It's brilliant in its simplicity. Petunia is actually a genius in this regard, but she still needs to do her assignment. Ultimately, it's the doing of the assignment, not the assignment itself that will bridge the gap between the learner she was in elementary school and the one who is ready for the challenges of high school and beyond.

Signed,
Someone who has done this more than once

This lovely if not wholly unpredictable two step—kids flail; parents freak out—is the dance of the middle school teaching team. For every missing assignment that stacks up, parents envision GPAs tumbling into freefall, college dreams disintegrating into unrecognizable crumbs, and basements filling with children forced to live subterraneously as a result of their poor life choices. Kids, for their part, tend to lie to cover their tracks, hide the evidence of their failings, and try to stay on the good side of their parents, teacher be damned. Then more emails ensue. But this is when any middle school teacher worth her dry erase markers shares the secret that lowers the temperature in the room (or in this case the email): Middle school is not the end game. It doesn't really matter. Like at all. And, also, thank goodness.

During the global pandemic, when I was up to my eyeballs in online learning protocols for students, this was a really soothing notion. At the time, parents and students alike were vacillating wildly between profound thanks for me and my fellow educators and a deep, abiding apathy that any of it mattered at all. I myself was self-medicating with copious amounts of bread. However, transforming standards and curriculum into meaningful lessons that could be delivered synchronously, asynchronously, in a Zoom meeting, or on a laptop was a circle of hell even Dante could not have imagined.

I was tired in a way that made even simple acts, like picking what to choose next on Netflix, difficult. I reminded myself of the argument that while middle school is transformative and important, it is not a full stakes game. In fact middle school is where you are supposed to falter and fall, experiment with different personas, and generally just figure out a way through. Middle school is actually one of those stages where it's the journey more than the destination that counts.

Herein lies not just the great enlightenment that will illuminate the passage through middle school with your child, but the joy as well: Colleges do not look at middle school transcripts. Whoo-freak-ing-hoo. Administrators at institutions of higher learning know what we earnest parents haven't quite grasped: There is no time like middle school to learn a lesson the hard way. Many kids need to falter and fall to learn how to get from elementary school, where parents were largely in the driver's seat, to high school, where they should be. Now many a parent has argued, "If I don't help him, he'll fail." I argue back that failure is communication in its own way. Communication changes dramatically during these years for lots of reasons, all developmental and appropriate, so take any communication you can get, right?

In middle school, behavior communicates as clearly as language. Sometimes kids don't have the language to say, "I don't get this," or "I didn't have the time I need to do this," or "I wasn't listening." But failure communicates these messages loud and clear. Failure, while scary in our uber-competitive and achievement-oriented society, should be looked at as an opportunity to ask questions. The only stupid questions are the ones we need to answer but choose not to. The only real failure is not investing the time to teach this kind of reflective questioning. The short list of questions I ask students and parents to ponder:

Did I have the time I personally need to finish this? Why not? What can change for the next time?

Did I listen to instructions? Why not? What could I do next time to make sure I understand the assignment?

Did I ask for help? Why not? What barriers exist for me to get the help I need?

But also this: If you are still helping your child with the heavy academic lifting in middle school, you are communicating quite clearly a message you might not be intending. The message is "You can't do this." Or, almost worse, "You cannot do this without me." Believe me when I say that there are worse things you can do than let them stumble a little bit. You can *not* let them stumble at all.

So maybe my essay is really more of a letter.

Dear Parents of Middle-Schoolers Everywhere,

You are in a tough landscape right now. The path forward is a little rocky and uneven. Your kids feel the same. But there are things you can do. Make your home a place where kids can grow. Take time to walk beside them on the path. Reassure them that there is space for them to roam and dabble, sink and soar. Be grateful that despite society's push for ribbons and accolades, you know the truth and revel in the joy of knowing middle school doesn't really count. Let that knowledge give you the grace to forgive all the mistakes along the way. May you have some yummy snacks and tasty libations to ease your passage through this place. Godspeed.

Sincerely,
Teachers Everywhere

ERIN DYMOWSKI IS a mother of five, a teacher to many middle schoolers, and a writer when she has a minute. She writes with her friend Ellen Williams at *Sisterhood of the Sensible Moms*. Her work has been featured in *Huffington Post*, honored at BlogHer, and featured in several anthologies. As a middle school teacher and a mom who has now been through middle school five times, she considers herself not just fluent in Fortnite and TikTok, but rather skilled in curating the coolest memes. Middle school is where she spends most of her days and nights, so she feels lucky that she has lived to tell about it. She feels even more fortunate she found some words to shape that tale.

8

LET'S TALK ABOUT SEX

BY AMY ROSENBERG

I have the best teenagers. They don't smoke. They don't vape. They don't drink alcohol. They don't have sex. No drugs. Yes, I'm sure that my teenagers have never lied to me about these things. Why would they? I'm a cool mom and they don't have to lie to me.

Admire my coolness: When my teenagers were little, I used to tell them the most important thing to remember in life is to never drink too much tequila. And every night when I put them to bed, I said this: "Good night, I love you, I'm proud of you." (In fact, I still say this to them at the end of the day.)

I asked the other day if they recall what I told them when they were little about the one thing I wanted them to remember. Do you know what they said? They said I was always saying, "You can't be bored without being boring." How did that make it through and stick in their little brains but not my tequila lessons? How could they not say, "You always told us you love us and you're proud of us"? Sometimes I think they don't know how cool I am.

As a cool mom, I believe in fostering trust and self-sufficiency. As soon as my kids could do something, I let them do it. They could get themselves ready in the morning as toddlers. They could work the home tech devices by the time they were 6. They could pour themselves a bowl of cereal for breakfast and make their own lunches for school. I never made them do their homework. No! They learned the hard way what happened when they didn't do their homework—and they did it. I've given these kids the message that they are capable and that I trust them and that is why I'm proud of them.

However, my feelings of pride in their self-sufficiency changed when they became teenagers, because suddenly they had to learn about sex. That's something you really don't want your kids to figure out on their own. My oldest, a boy, has had the same girlfriend since eighth grade, so it didn't take long before I started talking to him more and more seriously about sex. I gave him condoms (which we threw out recently because they were expired). I told him to please discuss things with his father or someone before deciding to take any big steps.

And I guarded my house with security cameras and tried to track his every move. (Very cool. So cool.)

When my son hit 16, he started talking to me about wanting more alone time with his girlfriend. We live in a small town by the beach, perfect for teenage self-sufficiency in all kinds of activities. But one day he informed me that he was tired of going to the beach with her. He wanted time alone in our house. This proposal was a stretch, even for me. Of course he had never been allowed to bring his girlfriend to our house or her house without a parent home. I thought back to my teenage years. What was I doing with my boyfriend back then and how do we work this out?

Uh oh.

So I told him he could have her over while we were home, and they could be alone in the TV room. This seemed to satisfy him for a little while—until one day he had the nerve to tell me he wanted permission to be alone with her, in the house, in a room with a bed. IN A ROOM WITH A BED. He said that. I said, "Listen, I'm not going to just sanction you having sex in my house." And he responded, "Do you want me to have to do it in my car?"

I didn't know how to answer that because when I was a teenager, yes, if we wanted to do it, we had to do it in the car.

Anyway, one day I caught him sneaking his girlfriend into the house. Did I mention I put security cameras all over the place? I'm not sure why he thought I wouldn't catch them. Now I had to do something about it. If I didn't do anything, he would learn the rules were totally meaningless. But what could I do? He begged me not to tell his girlfriend's mom. By the way, the girlfriend's mom hates my son. Why, you may say, that cannot be! Didn't you start out by saying your teenagers are perfect? Yes, I did say that. But my son's girlfriend's mom is crazy.

No, she's not crazy. But she is crazy protective. She had her daughter when she was a teenager, and she is a devout Catholic. So of course she is doing everything in her power to keep her daughter from having sex, including attempting to keep her from seeing boys, thereby ensuring that her daughter is probably also going to get pregnant young. I go back and forth on this. On the one hand, I do not want my teenage son to have a baby. On the other hand, grandchildren!

Seriously, I believe the tighter the clampdown, the stronger the rebellion. Once, the girlfriend's mom texted me and said she wanted me to tell my son to stay away from her daughter because her daughter is a big liar. If there is one piece of advice I would give parents of teenagers, it's that you get to choose if your teen lies to you. If your teen can't live with your rules, they are going to lie to you. And this is actually a really serious problem because the last thing you want to do is teach your kid to lie! So I try to make rules my kids can follow. Look where that got me. I'm the parent who knows where my kids are, but I'm finding out that the girlfriend is lying constantly to her mom because she isn't allowed to have a boyfriend in the first place.

So I had to punish my son for disobeying my rule, and more so for lying to me about it, and now I had to worry about the girlfriend's honesty too. Dammit.

I thought about it for a long time and this is what I decided to do.

I gave them a choice: We would either tell the girlfriend's mom everything, or the two of them would have to sit with me for a sex talk. They picked the talk. Shocking, I know. The upshot of all my grand ideas: I was going to have two teenagers come over and sit with me while I lectured them about sex.

I realized right away that I actually couldn't handle a conversation about sex, so instead I told them I was going to ask them a series of questions that I wanted them to think about and perhaps talk about with each other later.

Here is the partial list:

1. How does it make you feel about each other knowing you're both willing to lie to your parents? Dishonest people lie. Are you sure that the other isn't lying to you?
2. Are you sure that neither of you has an STD? How do you know? Would you be comfortable asking each other to get STD tests? I would recommend you do this with any new person you are going to be naked with.
3. Do you talk about being physically intimate? Do you ask each other what the other person wants?
4. Son, are you sure you aren't pressuring your girlfriend? Girlfriend, do you know how to say "No?" Son, do you?
5. Do either of you worry that the other will break up with you if you don't let them kiss or touch you?
6. Son, are you willing to ask your girlfriend how she feels about you touching her body before you touch her? Will you communicate clearly what you want to do and be willing to hear how that makes her feel? Will you ask her what she wants to do and listen to what she says? How about the other way around—Girlfriend, are you willing to ask and to communicate clearly?
7. Do either of you think the other should have to do physically intimate things if they aren't comfortable, or if they are nervous or uncertain?
8. What would you do if you got pregnant? Would you have an abor-

tion? Do you know where the abortion clinic is? How would you pay for it? Would you have a baby?

THESE ARE ONLY a few of the delightful questions they had to hear me ask while sitting there next to each other, staring at me and trying not to laugh. By the way, my favorite thing about my son's girlfriend is that she's almost a year older than he is. She turned 18 a while ago and that day I breathed a huge sigh of relief. I mainly quit worrying about her mother. I figure anything she had a beef about after that was not my problem. Adult child, good luck!

After sitting with me for an hour, listening to all of these questions, including going over some of the content from a book called *It's Perfectly Normal*, which has a lot of interesting illustrations in it, the punishment was over. My son walked his girlfriend home.

A few minutes later he came back. I was sweating. My heart was pounding. *Was he never going to talk to me again? What would he say? What if she dumped him?!*

He came in the house and leaned down to give me the biggest hug. "Thanks, Mom," he said, "That was actually pretty good." He smiled at me and went to his room.

I really have the best teenagers.

AMY ROSENBERG LOVES LANGUAGES. She holds an M.A. and. B.A. in Linguistics and she speaks Japanese, German, American Sign Language, Spanish, and English. She lives on the edge of the world in Half Moon Bay, California, where she uses her language skills to write code and wrangle children. In 2007, she started a food blog called *She Eats!* where she chronicles her experiences with food and life. You can watch her old cooking videos on YouTube.

9

MOOD SWINGS: I LEARNED IT BY WATCHING YOU

BY CAT HOLLYER

Anyone who's met me will tell you I'm a moody em-effer. I cry at Tylenol commercials. I cry when I look at my dog. I cry at sunsets or my sweet husband's face. I'm basically always crying. It's lovely for everyone involved.

In the words of Ms. Gaga, I was born this way. I've been "too much" my whole life. My parents? Sweet and genteel, lovely and demure. They weren't yellers; they preferred whispering their disappointment at you. They used the right forks at the right times, consistently sent thank-you notes, and to this day remain emotionally appropriate, always. And then they had me, poor bastards. They put up with years of temper tantrums and drama. I once threw a wooden clog at a girl for saying I "liked" some boy. She got stitches; I got labeled a problem child. And my parents got to live with that embarrassment when all they wanted to do was sip martinis and not watch their children. (It was the 80s.)

But now they're laughing all the way to the bank, because I've officially been given something to cry about: preteen mood swings. One minute, laughs and smiles, the next, doors slamming. Hugs and snuggles, then locked doors and silence. I can go from "the best mom in the entire universe" (cue the crying) to "the worst ever I can't BELIEVE YOU WOULD EVEN DO THAT!" (Also crying.) And I have no idea how I accomplished either.

We've got a blended family with four kids, all preteens. We're just asking for it, really—it's Mood City over here. Just when we talk one down, another starts in with some end-of-the-world problem. I have a feeling we're engaged in a years-long game of emotional whack-a-mole. Sadly, no one will win and no one will get the giant stuffed animal.

Case in point: One night, we mentioned that a local restaurant had rabbit on the menu, then added, "Isn't that weird?" The next thing you know, our daughter was inconsolable. Another time, our son was distraught because I didn't get to watch him play video games for long enough. You read that right. Then there was the time I made my other son a sandwich and forgot to remove a piece of paper on a slice of cheese, and I "could have choked him!" ("Uh, make your own sandwich, maybe?") And then, there's our other daughter, who literally cried the other day because she was cold getting out of the pool. ("You know, there are kids who DON'T have pools.")

Now, I have no room to throw stones from my very delicate glass house. As previously stated, I have my own mental state to deal with. Part of it is the whole "blended family" thing. We're relatively new at it, and it is not easy. Someone once told me that blending a family is like making a stew—it takes a long time to come together, which I totally get. But it doesn't help when one kid or another decides to chuck some verbal jalapeños in that stew and screw everything up.

So just managing that takes up a lot of our day, not to mention my own anxiety and depression. Thanks to my best pal, Meds, they're mostly under control, but they still show up sometimes (see also: when no one thanks me for the dinner I just toiled over). Like any mental illness sufferer, I've gotta take time for self-care and exercise and the occasional nap. With all of this going on, how the heck am I supposed to pencil in my children's mood swings? "Let's see...I've got 6-6:15 open. Can you try to schedule your freak out then?"

That's the thing, though. Emotions are never convenient. They don't take a number; they cut right to the front of the line and demand to speak to a manager. They can be entitled a-holes like that.

And I get where my kids are coming from. Preteen years weren't kind to me, either. It was a rollercoaster, never knowing if I would just "be cool" from moment to moment. I was teased as a kid, sure, but I started taking it way too seriously starting at age 10. I could never crack the code of how to not get picked on, and it ate me up every single day—especially in junior high.

Junior high was this time when I felt like, "I'm finally gonna find my people!" And instead, I finally found new and more effective bullies. Everything I tried failed. I bought Calvin Klein acid wash jeans—they were the wrong acid wash. I listened to The Smiths—everyone else listened to Bon Jovi. All of my choices were wrong. I started avoiding people as much as I could, staying inside at recess to practice piano alone, because what was the point?

It escalated quickly. I started just wanting to disappear. Clearly, I wasn't good at life, I wasn't good at friendship, and without friendship, what was there? I would go for long walks and fantasize about what would happen if I just walked far, far away, never to be found. My mom would inevitably pick me up, after dark, down some unlit country road, and she would never ask why.

Then I made the mistake of telling someone that I was depressed and considering killing myself. Next thing you know, my whole homeroom class found out and literally made fun of me for *that*.

Eventually, I started studying this one book on our living room shelf—it was an encyclopedia of drugs and their interactions. I'd scour it for easily found items and check to see what I could mix with them to just eject out of this place. Sometimes I'd just sit and stare at the book, like, "Am I really gonna do this?"

I wasn't. And thank goodness. But to this day, when I look back on that period of my life, I have no idea what stopped me.

So maybe a big part of this mood swing problem is me. Maybe I'm projecting my own experience on to our kids. Maybe I'm worrying too much, wondering if each freak-out could lead to something devastating. Yes, preteen angst is annoying. Yes, I'm sick of the drama. But it's more than that—it's crushing fear.

Here's what I do know: Our kids are far more likely to seek out therapy than I was. I was never offered it, though clearly I needed it. It just wasn't a thing back then, at least not in my family. But our kids? They hear about it all the damn time. Hell, my therapist lives two houses down and every time we pass, they hear me extol her virtues. "That's the lady who keeps me from freaking out, kids!"

I've got to believe that normalizing mental illness for them will help. That the fact that we don't shy away from tough discussions will do something to help them feel heard and understood. That I've been through it and can show them my metaphorical scars will make them feel less alone. I've got to believe that, because what else is there to do?

If we've built this blended family into a safe place where people are comfortable losing their shit on occasion (or, if you're me, more often than that), then I guess we're doing it right. Even if there's a lot of door-slamming and yelling and crying in the process.

And so, to my family, I say this: Let's all be moody bastards together. Let's let it all hang out. You can roll your eyes at me, I'll roll mine at you, it's totally cool...and in fact, it's better this way, trust me. We might annoy the crap out of each other, but at least we'll be fully actualized humans who don't grow up to murder people because we never got to express emotions.

Because the last thing I want to do is raise a Unabomber. Clog-throwing has nothin' on that.

CAT HOLLYER IS KIND OF ALL over the place—she's a writer, musician, voiceover artist, and mom. She writes full-time for Hallmark and has written several children's books including *Nana Says No!* and *Mr. Bean: The Rule-Breaking Pup* and *The House Full of Love* (all proceeds for that book went to Ronald McDonald House Kansas City). She voices stuffed animals (yep) and ornaments for Hallmark. In her spare time she's part of the band Occurrence and writes essays for fun and profit(?). Follow her at @cathollyer_writer_of_things.

10

READING IS FUNDAMENTAL (TO RAISING TEENAGERS)

BY KIM BONGIORNO

When I close my eyes and picture my childhood, swooping back in time to compress myself into the space of my brain and body as it grew from little-kidness on up through teen years, I float into near silence. My bedroom, door closed but not locked. Long walks by myself for practical purposes. The backseat of my parents' car, lips sealed as I look out the window. Even when surrounded by others, I sat in compartments of my curious mind where thoughts and ideas swirled, their active growth muffling outside sensations.

If I had a childhood tagline, it would have been, "Why? Tell me everything." I *thirsted* for information. I had plentiful time on my hands to come up with questions that strung out from one observation, forming intricate webs, sticky and waiting for answers to cling to them, weigh them down. Problem was, I didn't have the resources to answer the relentless questions that filled the compartments stacked up in my head. I didn't get to ask them out loud. I, too, was near silent.

Normally, kids go to their parents for this sort of thing, but much of the subject matter I pondered wasn't of the ilk that mine would be willing to discuss. My much-older siblings were already gone from the house. We didn't have cable TV for me to access—not that I got to control which program could be on, anyway. The internet wasn't a thing. Interrogating the neighborhood kids on embarrassing or philosophical questions wouldn't have ended well. So I was left with two options: observations and books.

One thing I could count on with a mother who loved reading was a once-a-week trip to the center of town, where we'd swing by the library after running errands from when I was about 8 years old on through my high school years. She'd let me wander the children's section on my own, and I'd wait just long enough for her to get lost in indecisiveness by the mystery novels before taking action. There was information to be sought, and this was my opportunity.

I'd creep up the carpeted staircase with a few books under my arm, pretend to peek at the movie rentals available by the front door, then pause at the massive unabridged dictionary. When the ancient librarians were distracted, I'd pull a list of words from my pocket to look up their definitions. Ones I had overheard on the news, that my parents' visitors let loose before realizing I was still in the room, saw scribbled like graffiti in school bathrooms and under bleachers, or found in the books I read that didn't have enough context clues for me to figure out on my own.

After the final word, I destroyed the list and sprinkled it into the bathroom wastebasket as I made my way back to the stacks where my mother expected to find me.

With all the new definitions secretly sinking into my skin—some more illicit than others—I checked out as many different books as I could before the visit was over. While the selection wasn't particularly diverse, it was plentiful enough that there were some stories I had to tuck between more benign paperbacks in order to avoid them catching my parents' attention. In my quiet bedroom on a fading lavender bedspread, I read everything I could to learn everything I could. I read about being like me and not like me. About tragedy and hope. About grief and adventure. About where kids can go once released as legal adults from the environment they grew up in.

Each week, I took what I observed around me and used it to help me find new words to look up, new books to read. Then I used those definitions and books to help me make higher quality observations. These words, books, observations fed one another, nourishing me through adolescence. They built on one another, providing strength and structure. They did the same for me, giving me a better life as I grew, inside and out. They helped me become something better than I could have without them.

I read to get ready for periods and relationships. I read to understand why people did what they did. I read to feel laughter in my belly on hard days. I read to feel peace in my heart on even harder days. I read to know how to act at school dances and other social gatherings. I read to answer my questions. I read to come up with better questions.

Books helped me better understand myself, my surroundings. What I did and did not want. The people around me and those who never were. They were vital to forming who I was during my first dozen or so years as a reader, when empathy, opinions, biases, interests, and other important facets of who we are become honed before we leave our childhood homes.

Once I was 18 and out on my own, I didn't have the time or energy to be fed the same way. The webs of questions still wove in my brain's compartments, filling them until it was impossible to see one side from the other. I was good at ignoring them, ignoring the ache of curiosity, to focus on more practical things. I would get to that later.

Sometimes I'd accidentally stumble into my own head, and see all the yearning for more, feel the desire for information, education, understanding. My cheeks would flush with shame at all I knew I did not know. Well-practiced reflexes would drag me out and slam the door again, for there is always a hierarchy to what one should or can pay attention to at any given time. Survival first. Everything else later.

"Later" took over two decades.

Now a parent, I answered a relentless peppering of *Why?* from both kids all day long, and I loved it. It was a gorgeous noise, the constant Q&A sessions by my gloriously inquisitive offspring. Once they could read, I began reading again. Looking up words again.

Reaching into those web-filled compartments in my head to assure them that though I could only pull one thread of my own questions at a time, I was getting to them now. I was getting to them all.

Cracking open books for tweens and teenagers as an adult was a revelation. The authors and subject matter were more diverse, inclusive, honest than they were back when I was growing up. They, too, had a gorgeous noise they were unashamed of. My old and new questions were answered between the pages, unspooling my webs at a blinding speed, and it became clear that reading the same books as my kids was the best parenting tool I never knew to ask for. The voices, the stories, and the new lenses they gave me for my observations gave me strength and structure once more. They made me a better mother. They helped me raise my kids into people who were something better than I could have without them.

I did not see that coming.

Reading books with them as tweens laid a foundation of responding to questions that sparked up, whether it was to define a word, grasp a new interpersonal concept, or familiarize oneself with a moment in history. It made thinking with eyes and minds wide open the norm during our important years of development: theirs as kids and mine as the one guiding them. It got us into the habit of asking without fear, answering without judgment, working through things together or allowing someone to figure it out on their own.

Sharing books with them as teens added fortification to their beliefs, gave them the tools to use what they learned, experienced in the stories—fiction or non—as guides on how to move forward on their own. They're now old enough to spend more time without a parent to assist, but comfortable with that because of discussions we've had, information we learned together, perspectives we witnessed in the wide array of books we both enjoyed reading.

Because of books and our ongoing dialogues about them, I know my teenagers are more ready for this world and their places in it than they would have been without them.

I know they are in good practice of listening to other voices, believing unbelievable stories, doing the work to better understand people unlike them, which in turn helps them better understand themselves.

I know they see how much they deserve to live, thrive, and help others do the same.

I know they are allies to people marginalized or negatively targeted due to their identity, gender, body type, race, religion, culture, or other reason, are willing to stand up for them, and open to get better at doing so.

I know they have learned many essential pieces of our world's past that history books glossed over, left out, or miscredited, giving them a clearer perspective on how to do right in the future.

I know they have related to stories of other teenagers like them, normalizing the typical bumps along the road of adolescence.

I know they've witnessed positive models for teen romantic relationships, including matters of consent and respect.

I know they recognize toxic masculinity, how to not participate in it, how to deflect it, and when to ask for assistance with it as needed.

I know they are willing to look for magic—or make it happen for someone else.

I know they are not blind to the violence and abuses happening in our world, and how not to inflict that on anyone, including themselves.

I know they've taken the journey with characters as they navigated grief, loss, trauma, pain, recovery, healing, hope, love, and joy.

I know they've followed the untangling of all sorts of problems as they were solved, seeing what worked and what didn't.

I know they understand why so many stories are about uprisings, and how messy they can get before the dust settles over a better world.

I know they see the benefits of enjoying something simply for the pleasure of it, letting themselves laugh out loud with abandon.

I know they believe in the value of sharing their feelings and experiences with others, talking about them honestly, and bonding over the process.

I know they are people I genuinely love spending time with, and will miss when they move out—but I do not fear the silence returning once they do.

Thanks to the relationship with books my kids and I have had over the years, I feel confident that no matter where they are, I will always have the beautiful noise of stories to wrap myself in. I also believe that no matter how old they are, we will comfortably fall back into the habit of finding each other with new stories we want to share, to which the immediate response will be, "Why? Tell me everything."

~

KIM BONGIORNO IS the author and freelance writer behind the blog *Let Me Start By Saying*. A crafter of everything from funny parenting tweets (@LetMeStart) to fantastical fiction, her work has received praise from the likes of *Buzzfeed*, *The Today Show*, *Huffington Post*, and The Erma Bombeck Writers' Workshop.

KIM LIVES in New Jersey with her family, who are wonderfully tolerant of her book hoarding tendencies. Learn more at kimbongiornowrites.com.

11

RAISED WITH GRACE
BY NICOLE FELTZ

Teenagers... ugh!

My favorite line was "Just wait till they become teenagers." So snarky.

I would hear that all the time and not truly understand what it meant. I'd just smile and think: *What an asshole. That is your child you are talking about.*

I was young when I had Grace, my almost 16-year-old, and I had been through a shit ton of bad life experiences and made incredibly dumb decisions, such as a weddings, divorces, and engagements to all the wrong men.

I see my teenager now and think how incredibly different we are. I was boy-crazy and loved school and social activities. She has two close friends and just wants to play soccer. She doesn't love high school, doesn't want to be on committees, doesn't want to go to events early and talk to friends—maybe because her phone is attached to her fingertips.

I recently found my senior year scrapbook. I spent hours looking at all the pictures, laughing at some of the crazy stuff my friends and I did. We were so carefree. We weren't scared; we were adventurous and loved doing stuff together.

We didn't have to-do lists. We didn't time block. We just got out of school or practice and met up. We flew by the seat of our pants.

I miss those days.

It made me think of my teenager. She is in that part of life when things are fun, without responsibilities or bills. I want her to create those memories. I want her to have a part of her life that is fun! I want her to put the sunroof back and just drive down the highway, crappy music blaring and hair whipping in her face.

Because in all honesty, my heart breaks a little for this generation. They are having to grow up so quickly. Active-shooter drills, cyber bullying, suicides, and the pressure to have life planned out and be the best! They are cracking under all the pressure.

When I was in school, I didn't feel like if I picked the wrong major in college it was all over! I thought, *heck I'll switch majors if I don't like these classes.* But the pressure for this generation to know what they want to be, what college they are going to, and which sports team is the right one—it all started SOOO young for them. Everything from the time my daughter came out of my vagina was a race. Is she walking yet? Is she talking yet? Do you have her in a sport yet? What club? Is she taking college courses yet?

It's like STOP.

True happiness. That is what my teenage years were. Not money. A full tank of gas, friends, and an open road were joyful.

It was tough some days because girls weren't the nicest and you had to learn to stand up for yourself and others. You had to learn to decide who you were, and let's face it, we are all still trying to do that. With COVID-19, riots, politics, racism, the women's movement, and everything else that is spinning out of control around us, it's hard to get footing about your stance.

I guess somewhere along the way I did something good because Grace has the kindest heart. She has loved all of the foster children that have been in our home and she is above and beyond protective over her little sister, Meah.

I see her teach Meah, help her with her shoes, tell her how beautiful she is in her dress, play games with her, create Playdoh animals, and read to her. Instead of her little sister being a pest, she includes her. Grace's soccer team calls her the mascot! She runs over and sits in all the team meetings. My heart bursts wide open with love when I see that.

So I guess what I've learned about raising a teenager is that they are just as confused as we are. They just don't have the failures to reflect on. They are trying to find their way and have a ton of big decisions to make that determine their future. So I will continue to practice grace, patience, and understanding. Continue to teach her to be a good human and love hard because those are two qualities that will ALWAYS guide her to make the right decisions with her future.

NICOLE FELTZ IS a writer from Overland Park, Kansas. She is a wife, mother to two girls, and a passionate advocate for foster care. She performed in the 2016 Lawrence, Kansas *Listen to Your Mother* show. This is her first published piece.

12

HIGHBROW TEENAGE ANGST

BY HOLLY RUTCHIK

No one can raise an eyebrow like a Rutchik girl.

In rage, disgust, curiosity, or judgment, the eyebrow raise is an art form my four daughters inherited from the elder generation, which (somehow) now means me.

My own eyebrows have been a source of pride throughout my life. I use them to convey humor and self-deprecating punchlines onstage and behind microphones. As a wife and mother, I use them to express dissatisfaction with my husband and children. It was only fitting that, as I had one baby girl after another, they each showed me that they too were capable of the one-brow raise of curiosity and the furrowed brow of disgust. My own idiosyncrasies became less appealing when used against me by small, walking mirrors who shared my DNA.

Our eldest daughter's steel blue eyes sit dramatically and naturally under dark, perfectly peaked brows. As an infant, these brows gave away her mood, which was almost always cheerful and bright.

As she grew older, she used them to emote onstage, just as I had. After a particularly lively eyebrow performance of "Joy to the World" at the holiday concert, a group of mom friends commented on the "made for the stage" expressions of our daughter.

"Did you teach her that?" asked a friend who knows my love of theatre.

"No!" I scoffed. "Of course not! That's insane. Who would make a young child practice singing with their eyebrows?!"

Me, that's who! I'm a liar. OF COURSE I had her practice that way. That's what a true performer does. Use what you've got and all of that.

Her performance that year led to her being cast as the Virgin Mary in a funeral. The woman who ran the annual Christmas pageant passed away, and the community wanted to honor her by having children reenact the procession of the pageant during her funeral.

"It's a very important job, sweetheart," I said when the phone call came in. "Do you think you can remind everyone of the joy this woman brought to the community through her work in the Christmas pageant?"

"Of course I can, Mommy!" she sang. "I love bringing joy to others."

It was one of those perfect parenting moments. Those rare slivers of time when all seems right in motherhood, and I had done the world a favor by procreating. Slivers of time are just that, though: tiny and fleeting, leaving you wanting more.

I've always been "Mommy" or "Mama." I'd naively held delusions of always being called "Mama" or "Mommy" and never moving into the "Mom" title. There are entire franchises of the Real Housewives of grown women (draped in diamonds and more money than they know what to do with) calling their mothers "Mama." As with all the *Real Housewives* shows, they had me asking, "If they can do it, why not me?" I would be "Mama" until they put me in the grave. Then, after my passing, I would still be Mama, but with a "She's watching me from heaven," the sign of the cross and a kiss to the heavens whenever my name is mentioned.

However, I'm raising smart girls. This is a good thing for the world, not so much for my heart or my home. By the time the tween years hit, our eldest found a loophole. She began referring to me as "Mother" in front of others. Apparently, *Little House on the Prairie* pioneer language is less embarrassing to her than "baby" language.

And then it happened. Our eldest daughter marked the entrance to her teen years by a sneak, public attack.

After one of her performances, she welcomed me backstage to meet her new friends from the show.

I stood in a circle of young teen thespians with a stupid, unknowing grin on my face. She had invited ME backstage. I was the cool mom. The only one whose daughter wanted her to meet the cast. The one who is going to avoid all the teen drama.

And then, she stabbed me right in the motherhood. In public.

"This is my... mom," she said with a pause and a raised eyebrow that screamed "Please just roll with this here in public or I will die of embarrassment."

I'm not a total mom monster. I raised an eyebrow back at her, smiled and tried my absolute best to be cool, waiting until we were safely in the privacy of the car before laying in.

"So, thanks for introducing me to your friends," I said.

"I KNOW," she cried before I could even move into my planned mama guilt trip.

"Mo-om," she whined. "I mean, Mama, I mean, Ahhhhh! I HAD to!" she shouted. "I am literally THE ONLY person in my class who still calls their mom 'Mommy.' I CANNOT."

I figured this would happen someday. I was thinking it would be well into the teen years and not at the very beginning. I was sure her outburst of anger and my disappointment and guilt was a scarring teen incident my child would be paying for her entire life. As is our fashion, it was a dramatic entrance into the teen years for us. One I wasn't prepared for nor ready to handle.

I changed the subject with a calm "Let's revisit this when we aren't so upset" and then redirected her from the conversation (as any good mother does) with the bribe of her favorite takeout place for dinner.

Since she was able to write, we have shared our mother/daughter bond through little notes and encouraging quotes sent back and forth. We aren't snugglers, but we can both get behind an inspirational quote.

Late that night, I emailed her a quote about how important it is to say what you need and what you are/aren't comfortable with. It was my concession speech. She reciprocated with a "Make today the best day of your life" note left atop my computer.

That week, she took a "Who is Your Celebrity Twin?" quiz on *Buzzfeed* and reported back "Kim Kardashian." The theatre incident wasn't a one-time thing. Times were officially changing. I was parenting a teen. A teen *girl*, nonetheless.

I'm basically mom-ager Kris Jenner over here: almost half a dozen kids (most of them girls). I'm all for finding your voice, owning your truth and businesswoman success. However, I'd like to keep it off the internet and confined to the stage, or something fancy like science. My husband would say the nunnery is a good place for our daughters to find a fulfilling life. We still have kids wetting the bed. We're still working out the details and aren't ready for a child to be doing all the teenage "finding themselves" stuff already.

As our first child officially rounded the corner to the teenage years, I knew what I had to give her for her birthday.

I threw her a VSCO-girl themed party and filled a basket with all the "grown-up" things I knew she would like. I cried as I put the basket together. However, I found the strength to swallow the tears and sport a beaming smile as she opened each item. I refused to be the mother who can't let go of her child and stunts them or gives them nightmares or becomes the reason they can't hold down a job because they were forced to say "Mama" for forty-five years. I wanted her to know that I saw her maturing, and I was proud of her and happy about her new stage of life. I'm right beside her, and maybe even willing to walk behind her if she wants to walk alone for a while.

So, some of my favorite Real Housewives still call their mother "Mama." Those women get paid to fight with one another on TV like children. My kids know public squabbles mortify me and that a raised eyebrow means "Stop now or you'll hear it from me as soon as we return home."

That night, as my not-so-little girl hugged and thanked me for her birthday, I reluctantly handed over one last gift. It was one of the most emotional gifts I've ever given.

It was a handwritten note—from me to her—about how special and important she is to me and how, on this day, she gave me my motherhood, something I treasure even in the hard moments.

I signed the letter, "I love you all day, every day. All day and all night, Mom. P.S. Yes, you read that right. You can call me 'Mom.'"

She raised her perfect eyebrows, flashed me a stage smile, and leaped into my arms.

Now, she lives in the basement like a vampire, only coming above ground when forced to emerge for food. She sleeps until two in the afternoon. Her communication with her siblings consists of a sound that I can only compare to barking. And, for someone who can win the expression award for onstage projection, she seems to magically turn into Eeyore inside the walls of our home.

Just when I think I've lost her to her newfound teenage melancholy, she gifts me with intentional, written love, just as I do for her. The last sighting of my girl who "loves bringing joy to others" was found in the contents of a note left on my pillow. "You're doing great, Mommy."

The "Mommy" was underlined for dramatic effect. After all, I raised her right. Without a little flare for the dramatic, she wouldn't be my daughter.

～

HOLLY RUTCHIK, M.A., is a humor and inspirational writer and speaker whose work has appeared in magazines, websites, and books. She has contributed to book anthologies including the *Cup of Comfort, I Just Want to Pee Alone,* and the *Chicken Soup for the Soul* series. She is a columnist penning two monthly columns: "Minivan Matriarch," covering the adventures of being a working mother raising a "million" kids, and "OverBOOKed," a book recommendation column for busy women. Holly believes in words for encouragement. She lives in Wisconsin with Mr. Minivan Matriarch and their kids. Hang out with @rutchikholly on Instagram or find her at hollyrutchik.com.

13

OF HOODIES AND LEGENDS
BY K. BECK

I t wasn't his first, but it was his favorite. Mini Boden, forest-green with the outline of a Jolly Roger in bright orange thread. On a 3.5-year-old it boldly proclaimed preschool badass pirate. He wore this hoodie on the daily—alone in cooler weather and under a winter jacket when it was cold. To see our little round boy, all grins and puffy cheeks, march down the street with confidence filled my mama heart. He was confident and proud wearing that skull-and-crossbones, an almost cartoonish symbol of malice. Since grown-ups got to do whatever they wanted and it didn't seem fair, the fantasy worlds of superheroes and knights, of cowboys and pirates, let a little kid rule the world for once.

Eventually he outgrew his green Jolly Roger hoodie. I looked for a larger size, but they were sold out. Apparently everybody wanted a part of that Mini Boden swagger. We moved on to Batman, Spider Man, and Star Wars (a blue one he wore exactly two times before it departed to the land of the lost, much to my great annoyance, but *c'est la vie*). Now, as a tween, soccer chic is more his style.

What wasn't to love? Hoodies were warm and cozy, and made a statement to boot. A good hoodie had the power to make you the boy you wanted to be.

In our neighborhood, I noticed exactly how teenagers of all races rocked their hoodies: for fashion's sake, warmth, or a combination of both. It wasn't hard to figure out that if you were a Black kid, maybe a hoodie made the wrong statement, marking you as someone who was up to no good and needed to be taken down, even if you were still a kid.

A hoodie was why Trayvon Martin, an innocent and unarmed Black 17-year-old coming home from the store with some iced tea and Skittles, was murdered. His hoodie served as evidence of criminal intent in the bullshitstorm of the murderer's mind, conjuring up a big black monster capable of unspeakable violence instead of a teen holding some snacks. *Don't wear a hoodie* was etched into the 21st-Century version of the Black Codes, a list of rules that white people are almost pornographically shocked by. A list that BIPOC can never follow too closely because Mr. Charlie would change the rules on a whim, and our Black lives literally depended on keeping up with those whims. These rules were passed down through the generations, evolving, but never disappearing, over the years.

I never looked at a hoodie the same way again. On the danger scale, it was a few steps above a water gun, something my kids knew they were NEVER EVER to play with outside the walls of our home. But I wanted to keep my son's innocence for a while. I rationalized that he could still wear a hoodie, as he wasn't even in kindergarten. How could anyone be threatened by my sweet little guy?!

We had time to preserve his innocence, didn't we?

Time before he'd be seen as a threat, right? But how much?

Ever since the day our children took their first steps away from us, out of the room and down the hall, we've walked the delicate line between letting them be joyfully free, making them proud and strong, while staying mum about the realities of being Black in America. When I'm around helicopter moms who treat their kids like Waterford crystal, I burn actual calories from eye rolling and withering glances. But there was a big difference between tripping and falling at the park and getting shot in the chest or beaten to a bloody pulp by some sickfuck of a racist cop or vigilante who truly believed that any Black person was a threat that required a weaponized response no matter their age or innocence. Tamir Rice was 12 (12!) when he was shot for playing with a toy gun in a playground. You can't protect a Black child, or any Black person from racism, because it is everywhere.

It. Is. Everywhere. Even when the news outlets haven't covered the latest incident. Even when our inner circle of friends seem at ease.

The murders keep happening. Children like Aiyana Jones. Teenagers like Michael Brown, Freddy Gray, and Jordan Davis. Women like Sandra Bland and Atatiana Jefferson. Grown men like Philando Castile, Alton Sterling, and Eric Garner—a dizzying and grossly incomplete list. So many names that, like mass shootings, you can't remember which is which. So many killed and so many murderers acquitted, producing a rage that turned to numbness. Now, in 2020, Ahmaud Arbery, Breonna Taylor, and finally George Floyd: gone.

And the nation exploded.

The list above is just a fraction of the murders that made the news. Other killings didn't make the national attention cut. Between Black family and friends, stories about the police remained anecdotes, the pain and fear recast into spiritual, if not physical, scars. When most white people heard these accounts, they'd think, *They must have done something?!* Of course that's what they thought. Between the headlines, and the photos of the victims and perpetrators, that's how the media portrayed the stories. The World of Whiteness, compared to ours, was like a fairy tale, where the police protected and served YOU, and usually did so with respect. Because if this is what you are fed from your society from birth, of course you insist there must have been a good reason to hurt, or even kill. It just doesn't make any sense otherwise.

It just doesn't make any sense to us either. But in a different way.

Remember the Charleston, South Carolina massacre? Nine innocent Black people at a Bible study were slaughtered by a racist lunatic. Once apprehended, the police bought this psychopath a fucking burger!

He murdered nine innocent Black people and was treated like a hungry, neglected puppy. Countless unarmed Black people, men in particular, have been killed on the spot by police or vigilantes without even committing actual crimes—and definitely without a stop for take-out. Let that sink in.

Black people have tales-a-plenty of overaggressive policing: the policeman who tackled a 12-year-old innocently shopping at the mall because he fit the description (we all look alike, right?). Or maybe the cops trained guns on a Black person because they had the audacity to have friends in or actually live in a nice (white) neighborhood. Or the cops didn't like that a nigger owned an expensive car, so the Black driver was cuffed, lying face down on the pavement like an animal, while their vehicle was searched. Being detained, humiliated, sometimes even beaten or tortured, fearing for our lives—never an apology when nothing is found—just because.

Because why? Because those fantasy worlds little kids invent, the ones where a superhero has all the power, that's all too real for white people who live lives so tainted by racist messaging that they don't know anything else, and don't even think to ask questions. Corrupt police, self-appointed vigilantes, and people just itching to call the police on some Black person for egregious behavior like sitting in their parked car get to play out their delusions of superiority in a world that tells them they can do no wrong.

Justice may be blind, but it sure as hell favors whiteness. The perpetrators of these disgusting acts know this and take every advantage of their presumed innocence and a Black person's presumed guilt. The power sure must feel good, especially if the perpetrators feel powerless in other parts of their lives. These trash humans come from an alternative mind-frame where they are incapable of, or even deliberately refuse, to see Black people as humans. They see them only as criminals or animals, as though they are stuck in the antebellum mythology of the besieged plantation mistress and her gentleman planter savior. Breaking News: It's not 1850, and you're not on fucking slave patrol. It's time for Massa and Lady Call-The-Cops Cooper to join the 21st century—to lose their inane and dangerous visions of themselves and of Black people, visions that make Black life a minefield. Visions that put the innocent children of moms like me at risk.

Little kids move on from their knights and pirate phase. Maybe more white people need to outgrow the idea that their whiteness gives them dominion over the universe.

A part of me wanted my now tween boy to wear his hoodies loud and proud all up and down the street and wherever he went. I hated that one more pleasure would be denied him because of the delusions of whiteness, a relentless message that any Black person is inherently criminal or otherwise unworthy. It was stupid and unfair that even on cold Chicago days, my son knew that he couldn't put his hands in his pockets and had to wear a hat instead of his hood. *It's right there!* All warm and easy to nestle into, but it's too dangerous for him to do so.

I tried not to hound him too much, but the second he'd put the hood over his head and his hands in his pockets, his dad and I would freak out. "Take off the hood and put your hands down!" I'd hiss, when what I really meant was, *I'm terrified that someone will see you, my baby, as a threat and hurt you.* I was angry at myself for being afraid, although I had every reason to be, because having your Mama around didn't mean a thing to the wrong cop. Why would it when there were zero consequences—when they could wake up the next day and do it again?

At least on the outside, most tweens and teens look surly AF. They can appear mean, eager to mock you, or worse, just for grins. I didn't like teenagers when I was one, but hoodies somehow rewrote the story on how this singular group of learning and growing humans was treated by the people in charge.

No matter how much of an asshole a white kid was, a hoodie was just a piece of clothing, without indication of criminal intent, character flaws, family income, or anything else. Whatever he did, he'd get away with a slap on the wrist, certainly less than a boy with darker skin. "Boys will be boys" is the automatic excuse used in the defense of their behavior, no matter how harmful or harmless it was.

But a Black boy in a hoodie couldn't get away with simply existing while Black. His hoodie was looked at as an automatic tell, one that pointed to ill intent. Guilty until proven innocent, which often didn't happen until post-mortem, if at all.

For a teen, a hoodie served as a soft and comforting refuge. When being lectured by their parents, something likely suffered often by angsty teens experimenting with pushing boundaries, a hoodie let a teen burrow deep down into it like a turtle into its shell. What a perfect escape from parents' word vomit of scolding and directives. I thought it was a phenomenon that affected just my boy-man, but I've talked to a diverse group of friends and learned that my son is in good company. In fact, since my son was doing this so much as a way to tune us all the damn way out, his dad and I had an excuse to take his every last hoodie away.

They now live in my closet, to be loaned out and returned like a pair of bowling shoes. We'll have the summer off from this particular worry, but I can't say what will happen when it grows cooler again. I'll need to see less activity from Officer Trigger Happy and the folks who make a job out of calling the police on Black people for simply living, for just trying to BE. Yet one more time, I'll have to weigh the odds versus the ever-changing rules.

With pride and tremors of anxiety I watch my beautiful children grow into wiry tweens, all muscle and sinew. My son's voice is just beginning to drop, his shoulders are broadening; it's easy to see he'll be ripped. I celebrate the beauty of my daughter and son, while being scared to death for them. When I hear of the 1980s summers many of my white friends are giving their kids, letting them pack a lunch and bike all over creation like they're remaking *ET,* I can assure you that won't be happening here for a while. I know my tweens will have to grow up and navigate and experience the world on their own. It kills me that I have to train them to the point of muscle memory how to behave in the presence of people who refuse to recognize their humanity, let alone their individuality. All we can do is fight for change, hoping that very soon we Black mothers can watch our children walk off into the sunset in peace. And if that child is wearing a hoodie, our only worry should be if that hoodie is warm enough.

K. BECK EARNS a living helping people younger than she is stand up straight, stretch their legs and feet, and move in time with the music she is playing, as opposed to the tunes in a car driving down the road. The rest of her time is passed scrolling through social media and figuring out how to efficiently provide her family with their preferred foods from four different grocery stores. A BlogHer Voice of the Year Award winner, this is Ms. Beck's third anthology appearance. From the bottom of her heart and soul, she hopes we can rebuild the world our children so richly deserve.

14

I'M NOT LIKE A REGULAR MOM, I'M AN UNCOOL MOM

BY HEATHER REED

I've just had an epiphany: I actually like my son. And believe me, no one is more surprised to realize this than I am. Now hear me out. He's 14. And between pretending to understand pre-algebra and breaking up fights between him and his 8-year-old brother, we've been sheltering-in-place for the last three months with very little room to breathe. Amid the chaos and requisite daily screaming, I've caught myself having bouts of reflection. Maybe it's the unearthing of old photos and memorabilia, in my foolhardy, adult-onset-ADD fueled attempts to clear space during quarantine, but memory lane hits hard.

Like my mother before me, Kyle was born when I was 23. This was considered "very young" for the San Francisco Bay Area, and the only other woman in my circle who was close to me in age was 33. The rest were in their late 30s/early 40s having their first kid.

Despite my fledgling the-military-will-pay-for-rent-and-health-care-if-we-get-married marriage, I felt adequately prepared to be a mother. My own mother was an OB/GYN, and I was essentially raised on the L&D floor at the county hospital in Cleveland, Ohio. I'd been a nanny and wanted kids of my own from as early as I could remember. When I found myself accidentally pregnant one week after my engagement, I was shocked, but not distraught. My mom assured me that she'd either fly out to California herself and give me the abortion or help me raise my kid. I appreciated her candid nature and acceptance of this unexpected news. I decided on the latter.

Pregnancy was easy. The birthing process was a mismanaged disaster, but that is a story for a different time. After a four-day induction, and less than twelve-hour postpartum hospital stay, I was home lamenting the loss of my Christmas shopping window. Kyle was over three weeks early, and my biggest concern was not having the appropriate amount of time to transition my precious firstborn—a Pitbull named Miss Cleo—from the top of the bed to the bottom.

Breastfeeding was a dream. Co-sleeping was second nature. I was young and had a ton of energy. A phenomenon my 30-year-old self would come to resent the second time around. When I first discovered that things in my new reality were anything but perfect, Kyle was 3 months old, and I'd been up nursing on and off for hours before I remembered that my husband was actually home. He'd been locked in our—never to be a nursery—second bedroom, playing World of Warcraft for just over twelve hours. I had literally forgotten he was there and my deeply rooted hatred for video games comes from this place. Our marriage took about fifteen more months to completely unravel, but before it ultimately ended in a literal fit of rage and violence, the damage had been done. Kyle had witnessed his father hit me and take off, and he didn't see him again for nearly ten years.

Rage, loneliness, despair, more rage. Rinse and repeat. Kyle was mine. There was no one else present in our space (except Miss Cleo), and, well, he looked just like me. He came everywhere with me. I knew that having a well-travelled child who knew how to behave in restaurants was the most important thing to me at 25, and quite frankly, those things remain tantamount to my success in this parenting exercise.

By the time he'd turned 5, I'd remarried and we were on our way to becoming a whole family again. However, this union was destined to fail in a much uglier way that its predecessor, albeit without the physical violence. Watching his brother being born in a birthing tub on our kitchen floor was definitely one of the highlights of his young life, but that idea of our new family was short-lived. Kyle probably took this disappointment the hardest. I brought another man into our home. A man with whom I thought we'd rebuild our lives. And for a while, it was great. For a while, Kyle had a dad. The only man he'd ever called "Dad," in fact. And that man would go on to dismay and betray Kyle worse than the bio dad he barely knew. The part that gutted me more than anything was the fact that I knew this was my fault. I'd done this to him. To us. And it was up to me to rebuild him. To rebuild his trust and help him navigate this not-so-new normal that was just us. Alone. Miss Cleo had since left this earthly realm, and here we were. Unearthing new behavior patterns and coping mechanisms.

We have fought viciously, and I carry the wounds around with me from the handful of times I've lost my temper. He still flinches when he does something stupid and I react. It's not a traumatic flinching, but it does poke at me.

My son is an idealist, which seems kinda cute. But trust me. It is not. If I had a nickel for every time I was reduced to a pile of anguished rage due to some aggravating, precocious behavior, I would be "up to here" with nickels. But shit, if he can't see the good in all people while navigating next to impossible teenage BS. Few things have made me prouder than the times I've done a deep dive into his text messages. Now before you get all incredulous on me, *no*, I don't believe teenagers deserve privacy on the internet or on their devices. As parents of teens in the age of advanced technology, it is our goddamn duty to keep apprised of this content.

I am the uncool mom whose job it is to monitor and engage with strangers on social media, so I am acutely aware of the perils that await teenagers in this day and age. I find myself in an interesting and empowered position to have both been raised with computers, and have a child come of age during the iPhone era. The surprises that awaited me in his phone were not that of a degenerate porn addict, but rather those of some sage teen-whisperer. Girls pour their hearts out to him, and he responds with compassion and a wisdom that he has not fucking earned. Boys talk shit and get ridiculous, and his response is a resounding, "Bruh, gross" or some variation of that.

He is tender. He is kind. He is fiercely loyal and borderline co-dependent in his service to both me and his little brother. As the child of an addict, I always worry about this last part, but I hope that I can help him grow out of that by the time he graduates high school.

When we embrace now, his hugs are like a man's. He is nearly a full-grown human, and I have to check myself every time I think of leaning into that and treating him like an equal partner in the struggle, for he is neither my companion nor my helper. He is my son.

Also, I want to fucking kill him most of the time. Am I speaking in hyperbole? Of course I am—but these feelings wane in those dark and still moments when he aggressively flops his 140-pound self onto my half-alive Ikea couch, and gently rests his messy, unkempt head on my lap.

In those stolen and quiet moments, when I'm able to break myself out of the confines of my crippling resentment, I experience joy. And companionship. And love. A love that one may feel toward a growing young person that you simultaneously want to throttle and protect from life's ugliness. But you forget that they've already seen their fair share of ugliness, and despite the fight over dishes and homework, at the end of the day, you're all they have. And they're all you have.

They're the shitty teenager whose clothes are all over the bathroom floor, *again*, for some godforsaken reason, as though Jesus himself is constantly absconding with the laundry hamper in an attempt at some sick humor. "I forgottttt," he yells. And I die a little more inside.

And I have to remind himself that even though we've been through fire together, he's still just a kid. And maybe all of the pain and sacrifice has led us here—to the remaining four years of youth. And, forgive me as I hold back my vomit, maybe they should be cherished.

∼

HEATHER REED IS the Director of Social Media at *Lucie's List*, and a freelance Digital Marketing Director. She's lived in the San Francisco Bay area for seventeen years, though she remains loyal to the Cleveland sports teams of her youth. As a single mom of two boys (ages 14 and 8), she has maintained her Mother-of-the-Year status, in spite of the soul-crushing teen years that have befallen her as of late. She has a BFA in Photography from Syracuse University, yet she's managed to fill a 256GB iPhone exclusively with breastfeeding photos, Little League strikeouts, and other people's dogs. Follow her on Instagram at @HeatherOfTheYear.

15

A CAMEL, SOME STRAWS, AND YOUR COLLEGE-BOUND TEEN

BY ELLEN WILLIAMS

Your kid is a camel and you need to remove as many straws from their back as possible before they go away to college. Just stay with me a second. We've all heard "the straw that broke the camel's back" or maybe even more specifically "It's the last straw that breaks the camel's back."

As part of humanity in all its glory, we are all familiar with that last straw—oh so familiar. It's the coming to the end of a no-good-one-new-problem-right-after-another kind of day, and just needing to get that dishwasher chugging before you can collapse into bed. You're almost there. You've almost cleared that hurdle. But, but, but when you reach under the sink for the detergent, the carton is empty, and you begin to empty out your pent-up fermented anger upon every man, woman, child, dog, cat, and goldfish within earshot. Was the empty carton really a big deal? Not for an organized planner like you; there is a Costco-size drum of dishwasher tabs thirty-five steps away in the garage on the shelf labeled "D." But you are out of patience, done, toasted, wrung-out from all of that day's mental load crushing your cortex until all you have left is your primordial reptilian brain. And that lizard is pissed. And suddenly you are Godzilla throwing straws, breaking camels' backs, and revving up the adrenaline coursing through everyone's veins. No one is getting to sleep in the next hour. Day officially ruined, and maybe the next one too. The question is, if your reserves weren't so depleted, would the thoughtlessness of an empty detergent carton have been just a point to discuss later instead of the end of communal peace?

So back to your college-bound teen camel. Picture them with a basket on their back, and into that basket they must stuff all the fresh things they need to learn to live on their own at college. So much novel stuff to add: managing classes, navigating the dining hall, negotiating with a roommate, and building new relationships. These things equal a heavy mental load that hogs a lot of space in that metaphorical basket. So why, oh why, would you want mundane stuff like doing laundry, using a microwave, and waking up to an alarm to add pounds to that limited reserve for newness? Why make the distance from *happy camel* to *broken back* that much shorter? Let's also remember that one person's incompetence is another person's last straw.

Picture the scene. It's finals season and my daughter lays her weary head down at 1 a.m. after studying for hours. Slumber ensues pretty quickly because she is exhausted. A mere hour passes and when the clock strikes 2 a.m., the dorm fire alarm goes, "WAAOHAAA, WAAOHAAA, WAAOHAAA!" Strobe lights! Scrambling for shoes! Throwing on glasses! Realizing that finding glasses should have proceeded searching for shoes! Evacuation!

My daughter huddles outside with twelve floors of freshman and quickly scans for crocodiles; it's Miami, after all—and thank goodness since it's December. She sees messy buns, bedhead, and slightly askew boxer shorts. She sees students sprawled on the green with laptops and notebooks struggling with the dewy dampness and battery chargers. Thoughts and good vibes for those noble procrastinators unlucky enough to need just a few more hours of studying before those blue books get slapped onto their desks tomorrow, or rather later that day. She notices a firefighter talking to her friend Marvin (name changed to protect the Last Straw's identity). Marvin lives on the floor below my daughter. Marvin had decided he needed a snack to power through his Accounting 101 study guide, so he grabbed one of his roommate's Easy Mac microwavable macaroni and cheese cups.

Now, our friend Marvin's understanding of "easy" differs from that of the Kraft Corporation's. See, Kraft, and frankly many others, think it's easy enough to add water to that lump of pasta and neon cheese powder; but alas, Marvin has never reheated anything other than leftovers in a microwave. Therefore, instead of making a tasty glob of goodness, Marvin made a fireball that fueled the ire of 959 of his fellow students. This was more like a log than a straw; therefore, the sound of camels' backs cracking could be heard throughout the land.

Let us pause for my other daughter's contribution. Since I didn't use her microwave story, she insists that at the very least I emphasize that metal does not go into a microwave, including those foil takeout pans and the handles on Chinese food cartons. There are Marvins everywhere. Oh, yes there are.

But *you* don't need that tip. You are an accomplished adult who knows how a microwave, as well as many other things, work. Your household is a well-oiled machine. What you need is a nudge to consider why your household runs so efficiently. It's because one or more adults at your address are the gatekeepers, problem-solvers, clean-up crew, and tech support. You're the lube that keeps everything running smoothly, and it's time to let your teen cause some clunking. To wax poetic, it's time to let your kid grease their own gears.

Don't bristle because you think you're being dragged into a raucous round of "You've done parenting wrong." Nope. I am here to cheer you on to invite chaos into your life. It's not easy to give up control because your system is so good, but if you have ever muttered, "I'll just do it myself because it's easier," that is exactly the task you need to turn over. It's easy for you because it's so routine that it is like a program running in the background for you. Of course you don't want to turn it over to your teen because it suddenly becomes a whole time-sucking thing. It goes from being *mastered* to a straw in your mental load. But remember poor Marvin. His back cracked the loudest that night because the mundane wasn't mundane for him while he was cramming for his first round of finals.

Now the General of Defense in your brain may be hoo-hawing, "But MY kids have always had a chore chart!" Congratulations because you're halfway there! They've got skills; now they are ready for that promotion to management. For example, does your kid clean the bathroom, but you list every task, tell them when to do it, and put out the cleaners for them? Time to let them decide when to clean and what to use. When they leave home, life no longer comes with a checklist. They have to be the catalyst, momentum, project manager and staff. This may sound like some hyperbolic importance given to cleaning a toilet, but it's just an example that happens to be a very pertinent example because young adults love bleach. I don't know why. It's true that it kills the nasties, but it's unfortunate that it reacts with other very common cleaners to produce hazmat-level gas. Once upon a time a very bright girl completed her freshman year of college and thought if one cleaner really kills the germs then two is even better! Was it my really good friend who sparked the evacuation of a day camp in 1989 or my daughter's suitemate who cleared them out of their campus apartment in 2017? Answer: both!

I mean I couldn't resist the bookending bleach stories, but I cannot hit every pitfall of every task. Just maybe have your kid step beyond the checklists and take full responsibility for a few things. Have them plan a meal—from picking out the recipe and picking up the groceries all the way to assigning tasks to family members and then cleaning up. Have them do their own laundry. This is a task that cracks many a freshman because perhaps there are a few parents who think there is a perfect way to do it, thus they just do it themselves. Have your kid Google "color catchers," embrace that miracle of modern invention, and then have them do your laundry too. Just tell them to stay away from bleach. Bleach doesn't need to be a straw at all.

I realize I have covered a lot of evacuation avoidance. You don't find that in a ton of parenting books, but here's a sobering thought: Those might not even be the most important tasks to transition over to your child. You will make the most room in your kid's basket for new straws if you transfer tasks of personal care and responsibility over to them in a slow build up to college.

Things like making their own appointments. Will this take a million times longer than if you just did it yourself? Hell yes! They are going to have to cross check your calendar, and get you involved, but they need to do it. Thank goodness so many appointments can be done online because modern teens hate calling. But making an appointment by phone is going to come up. Even if the only grinding of gears you can stand is having them call for a dental appointment on the exact day and time you feed to them, it's beneficial. First, you're making them use the phone in the way Mr. Bell intended, as a calling device. That's huge. Second, you'll coach them in the words they need to use for such an interaction. They are second nature to you, but not so much for them. And lastly, maybe you can get in a quick lesson about how and with whom your insurance works. Nothing like getting a huge doctor bill because your college student didn't understand what out-of-network meant when they decided to go to urgent care for a strep test, and they "Didn't want to bother you."

Along these lines, have them keep their own calendars, and set their own reminders. It can be surprising how many kids just bob along like leaves in a stream relying on you to get them where they need to be. I dare you to ask a teen or two what they will be doing Tuesday of next week. There will be some blank stares. Also, have them monitor their own grades and assignments. You may have to take baby steps, like checking them together at first, then having them check in with you for a weekly meeting, then a monthly meeting, and then only when they need help. And for the love of schedule independence, have them get themselves up. I'm going to venture that a huge number of roommate conflicts could be avoided if "snooze" is only hit once. And just send setting multiple alarms back to their ring of Dante's *Inferno* where they belong. Both of my daughters have been blessed with various roommates who were accustomed to parents rousing them, so when I asked them for annoying alarm stories, it was a little incoherent, but "ARGHBJJJSYESH! . . . IT'S THE WORST!" sums it up.

The list of wisdom to impart could be endless. Just try to analyze how you grease the gears for your family and take opportunities to share responsibilities as they come up. Do things as momentous as letting them fly alone (or at least show them how to buy the tickets). Do things as ordinary as having them check over the restaurant bill for accuracy and calculate the tip. Just do it sooner than the week before they go away.

As in all things in life, timing is everything. If you wait until the summer before they go away to teach them how to change a tire, reboot the WiFi, balance a bank account, do laundry, scrub a toilet, and make your famous Chicken Kiev, you're not going to be removing any straws from their basket, you're likely going to freak them out. It's just not enough time to master these tasks into the background. They've got their own emotions, anxieties, and transitions they are working through. They've got orientation and class registration weighing down and taking up all kinds of room in their basket. My hard-won experience recommends opening up your School of Life early in the adolescent years. Of note, your timeline may be shorter than you think. Having been dragged through a couple of rodeos already, junior and senior year are pretty stressful, jam-packed years for college-bound students too. The receptivity of upperclassmen to adding even more to their plates can be somewhere between dismal and deaf wolverine.

Get them while they're young. Not only will they benefit, but your relationship will also. Many heart-to-heart talks happen while hands are busy, and eyes are focused on the task at hand. And you are leading them toward what your relationship will become: less project manager and more sounding board.

On Move-In Eve, as you lay awake going over all the things you wish you had taught your child, just know it never feels like enough, but you haven't crossed some finish line, just a "It's going to be different" line. There will be time for more life lessons. There will be more relationship growth.

To bring this full circle, remember you've got straws too. My wish is that your basket will be so light—because you know you did your best—that parking woes and falling cork boards won't even come close to being your last straw. I want you to enjoy the moment. And whether or not there are tears, you and your child will be bolstered by the confidence weaved into their being by your belief in their competence to manage their own life. That's the true magic of turning over responsibilities to your child—for both of you.

ELLEN WILLIAMS IS a copywriter and co-founder of the blog *Sisterhood of the Sensible Moms*, your source for sensible parenting advice delivered with humor and heart. She earned an M.D., but as it turns out, she should have heeded her high school teachers when they gave her the Senior Award for Excellence in Language Arts. She has worked as an OB/GYN intern, a college biology laboratory instructor, an event planner, a brand spokesperson, and an anthology contributor. With one daughter freshly graduated from college, and another one making her way through, her puggle and cat have lobbied for fur-baby status, but so far she and her husband have vetoed that. You can find her @sensiblemoms on Facebook, Instagram, and Twitter.

16

PARENTAL WHIPLASH

BY SUZANNE FLEET

My son Asher is so pregnantly teenaged at 12 years, 10 months, I feel like his body has suddenly been taken over by a crazed, incessantly hungry, emotional alien. Two weeks ago, he was a child. After so many years with him, I knew what to expect. He was sweet and loving to me and his dad, predictably irritable with his little brother, respectful to his teachers, discerningly nice to the dog and occasionally cried when he'd had too little sleep and too much homework. Mommy knew just what to do to make it all better.

For the latter half of 12, new sides of his personality have presented themselves. The first sign that changes were afoot was the daily occurrence of Cuckoo O'clock. Where once we'd had the "witching hour," when both boys went nutso right after dinner, wrestling with each other, bouncing off the walls and just kind of generally getting turnt up, now this same time of day is when Asher freaks out to the max. Describing Cuckoo O'clock is difficult. It involves loud, cackling laughter at—who knows? Sometimes there is something mildly funny happening but then it continues long after that funny thing has disappeared, as if the high-pitched cackle is eating and then throwing itself back up over and over with greater and greater convulsions. Often, it's just a meme he saw earlier in the day. He thinks of it again, throws his head back and lets loose. Even if he tries to tell us what's funny about it, we never get it. We mostly look at him puzzled and amused. We do not speak meme.

The emergence of Cuckoo O'clock was followed by the appearance of both a unibrow and a shadow of a mustache. Outward signs of imminent teen-hood were creeping in. While it's hard to get used to your baby boy growing body hair and becoming almost as tall as his mother, at least you know it's coming.

More surprising is the complete takeover of his body by the hunger monster. As a survivor of a sister-only kind of childhood where we girls predictably ate what I would consider "normal" amounts of food and then shamed each other about it, I'm confounded by my husband's descriptions of eating family-size cans of Chef Boyardee ravioli as an afterschool snack every day when he was a teen, especially considering he's probably never weighed over 140 pounds in his life.

He's told me these kinds of stories for years to help me understand there is no assuaging a teenage boy's hunger, not with two racks of ribs, not with an entire pizza, not with a bucket of chicken.

Still, I laughed internally when he tried to convince me that Asher would ever eat like that. Calling him a picky eater is generous. Ash ate a total of about eight things for most of his life. Even forcing him to touch his tongue to something outside of his range brought on immediate vomiting. For over twelve years, he lived on chicken nuggets, bread, peanut butter and jelly, cheese-sticks, pizza, strawberries, and only one specific brand of turkey slices. If you accidentally bought the oven-roasted turkey instead of the smoked, well—find someone else to eat it because Asher knows it's not the right one the second he tastes it.

But now that's he's swollen with 13, all bets are off. Not only is he suddenly willing to eat almost anything, he eats such vast quantities of food, he should by all rights weigh 835 pounds.

My husband made pancakes for my younger son Meyer and a friend one morning. Asher had a stack of them for *second* breakfast.

Twenty minutes later, he was back in the pantry munching on pretzels straight out of the package. It was 9:30 a.m.

Lunch consisted of five pieces of chicken, most of a family size bag of chips, an apple and an orange—more food than I consume in a single day. Watching him eat is like being at the zoo during feeding time. My growing lion tears apart the animal carcass, swallows great chunks of it whole and then looks up at me with glazed eyes like, "MORE MEAT!"

While I feel certain we're going to have to make a choice between feeding him during his teen years and sending him to college, there's some relief in seeing him widen his palette. He'll eat salad now, for God's sake. As long as you let him pour ranch dressing on it.

Another totally expected sign of teen-dom has been the retreat to his bedroom instead of hanging out in the family area all the time, and an awful lot of "listening to my music." His earbuds may become an actual physical part of his ears. Only time will tell.

But the strangest change has happened in just the last couple of weeks as actual 13 looms over us like a storm cloud. The mood monster has taken control of my son.

Just yesterday, Meyer asked him to turn off the showerhead at the end of his showers so he wouldn't get head-soaked when it was his turn. That seemingly innocuous request was denied with a dramatic "NO!" I then asked the little one to go back upstairs and tell Asher that it's simple common courtesy to turn off the showerhead when you're done. By his reaction, you'd have thought we'd announced that we'd given away all of our computers, TV screens, and phones, and were living out our new unplugged lives in the backwoods. He blew into my bedroom with slumped shoulders, his arms outstretched in a giant "WHY" gesture. He was sobbing hysterically.

"Why do I have to turn off the shower?" he said through gasps.

"Sweetheart, calm down. Do you need a hug?" I replied.

"Meyer is being a big jerk to me for no reason! Why is he always such a jerk?" He came in for the lightest of hugs, allowing me to put my arms around him but not reciprocating, his arms hanging limply at his side. Ash pulled away quickly and I felt rather than heard the pftpftpft as a small portion of the air in his emotional balloon was released.

How do you talk rationally to someone who loses their shit over being asked to turn off the showerhead?

I just don't recognize the person who is driving his emotional car right now. Because it's not the same person who was driving two weeks ago. Someone has surreptitiously slipped behind the driver's wheel and he is one TERRIBLE driver. He might even be blind.

There is so much swerving, so much random braking—speed limits are being discarded. There is random backing up, pulling forward then backing up again. Occasionally there are twenty-seven-point turns and even high-speed donuts. The person driving his emo-car has never been behind the wheel of a vehicle before but has decided, like the 5-year-old child who took his $3.00 savings and his parents SUV so he could go to California and buy a Lamborghini, that he is totally FINE to handle a 3000-pound car with zero experience, thankyouverymuch.

The problem with this is that I'm along for the ride and his new driving style is giving me parental whiplash.

Here's what I'd like to say to him, if I could: "Please pick a lane and stay in for a while. If you want to go into another one, look over your shoulder to see if it's all-clear and then signal, for God's sake. You're endangering everyone on the road right now with your schizophrenic Meemaw-meets-stunt-car-driver emotional style."

But if I said any of that, I'm 87% sure he'd start crying. Or maybe laughing. I literally have no idea who I'm dealing with anymore.

A few days ago, Asher spent time at a close friend's house. The two of them are "gamers" and while our electronics time rules are fairly strict, when he goes to his friend's house, we loosen them. At our house, he has to earn points by doing chores, reading, exercising and so forth, and then he can trade those points in for device time. After about five hours playing games with his pal, he came home and immediately asked to YouTube it for an hour.

"I've got enough points for an hour," he said, hopefully.

"No, you don't," I said, as if I was talking to a rational person. "You have to cash in those points for the five hours of gaming you did at Brewer's house."

In less than a second's time, his eyes turned fiery red like the devil and his head ballooned to four times its normal size. I took a step back. I wasn't sure what was happening.

"MOM! That's not FAIR!" he said. And then all of the energy in those eyes and head proceeded to gush through his tear ducts all at once.

"Umm, what is wrong with you, Asher?" I said, still unaccustomed to such outsized reactions.

"NOTHING IS WRONG WITH ME IT'S JUST UNFAIR OF YOU TO TAKE MY POINTS WHEN I EARNED THEM AND I JUST WANT TO GO TO MY ROOM AND CHILL OUT AND WATCH YOUTUBE FOR A LITTLE WHILE AND YOU SAID I COULD DO ELECTRONICS AT BREWER'S HOUSE AND IT WOULDN'T COST ME ANY POINTS AND NOW... DAD!!! MOM IS TAKING ALL MY POINTS!! IT'S SO UNFAIR!"

His voice cracked. The tears poured down his cheeks into his little caterpillar of a mustache.

Gabe and I looked at each other. One or both of us may have sprained our taints trying to control our facial reactions.

While watching TV a few days ago, we were all talking over each other as usual, cracking jokes back and forth. Asher apparently got cut off once or twice and then launched himself onto the couch, back arched like I haven't seen since his toddler days and yelled, "CAN. I. SAY. MY. THING. NOW. PLEASE?"

Everyone went completely silent and just looked at him.

At least he said please, I guess.

I know, I know. We were teens once. We shouldn't be so surprised by this rollercoaster of emotion. It's the sudden impact that has me reeling. I guess I expected it to creep in, not hit us with the impact of a high-speed car crash.

This almost-not-child is swollen with the promise of facial hair, girlfriends, zits, school dances, awkward first kisses, break-ups and all the other teen things he can feel ballooning inside him. The hormone sprinkler is going full blast inside his body, flooding every-thing, and no one, least of all him, can even adjust it.

But just when you think you're dealing with one of the more unreasonable humans on the planet, he happens upon your story about him on your open laptop, reads it and smiles slyly.

"I can't believe I cried about the showerhead," he says. "That was really cringe."

And this time, we laugh together.

~

SUZANNE FLEET IS the writer and humorist behind the blog, *Toulouse & Tonic*, and author of essays and short stories in numerous antholo-gies. Suzanne likes fancy cocktails, tie-dye anything, and can be counted on to say hello to dogs before humans. She is also forever working on her own book of essays that may or may not ever get done. You can find her @toulouseandtonic on all the social platforms.

17

SCREEN TIME

BY CANDY MICKELS MEJIA

I t was a win/win situation: I finally agreed to let her watch *The Office*, but on the condition that we'd watch it together. I'd seen nearly every episode when it was originally on, but Sophie was a baby then. The specific content and language weren't things I was screening. I couldn't fathom the idea of her being old enough to watch something that I watched, much less something I enjoyed.

And then she became a teenager.

We had to steal moments to make it work. Opportunities when my husband wasn't home and/or my younger daughter was distracted by whatever 9-year-olds are distracted by. Time was precious, so as soon as we knew we were in the clear, we both plopped onto the couch. One of us would grab the remote and click our way to whichever episode was next, both of us silent as to not miss a word of the cold open.

Binge watching a TV show with my teenage daughter was a parenting perk I didn't see coming. Laughing at the silly situations together while worrying about Michael Scott's ignorant optimism was a time for us to relax and recharge together, which isn't always possible with the busy-ness of life—and isn't always agreed to by sassy teenagers.

We were addicted to the show and to our time together, but then it was over. We'd finished all nine seasons with no plan of what to do during those brief windows of time we'd been seizing for ourselves. I didn't want to just let our little routine go. I worried that we wouldn't be able to make it happen again. Or worse—that she wouldn't want to.

Sitcoms have always been one of my favorite forms of entertainment. I never had a routine of watching them with my parents, but when my dad would watch them I was usually nearby—*M*A*S*H*, *Happy Days*, *Mork & Mindy*, *Sanford & Son*, *WKRP in Cincinnati*, *Benson*, *Bosom Buddies*—I'd catch bits and pieces of them from time to time. When I was just a little older, sitcoms were my after-school entertainment. Episodes of *Three's Company* and *The Jeffersons* have been imprinted on my mind forever.

None of these were watched on purpose, though. Either they just happened to be on or they were literally the only interesting thing on at the time of day I wanted to watch TV.

As I entered my early teenage years, around the age my daughter is now, sitcoms were all that was on primetime TV. I feel like I watched all of them, though I know that's not possible. Certain shows I watched more than others; I was a big fan of *Family Ties* and I loved *The Cosby Show*. I would have gladly accepted invitations to hang out with either the Keatons or the Huxtables. Lord help me, I was drawn to shows with tidy little lessons at the end.

Yet my favorite shows since I've been an adult were never tied up with a nice bow at the end of each episode. Instead they featured silly situations, sarcasm, and, often, really bad decisions. Watching all nine seasons of *The Office* alongside my teenage daughter, I noticed something else all my favorite shows have in common: humanity.

The Keatons and the Huxtables were literal families in the reality of their sitcoms. Mom, dad, siblings were all in the same house. They were obliged to care for each other and to forgive one another based on how "happy" families are supposed to act in our society. A peaceful resolution to whatever problem had come up was not a surprise; it was a requirement. In *The Office*, however, those obligations did not exist. The characters built intentional relationships with each other and bonded over shared experiences. Despite Michael Scott's need for attention or Dwight Schrute's obsession with power, these two oddballs had a real friendship. Though Jim Halpert endlessly pranked Dwight, they, too, had a strong bond.

After we finished *The Office*, Sophie and I started trading ideas of what other sitcoms we could watch together. *Parks and Recreation* was a natural choice since it's another workplace comedy, but I wasn't quite ready to dive into that with her. Upon my review of the episode list, I realized there were more adult situations than I'd remembered (thanks, "Tammy 2"). So instead we shifted gears, if only a little, and started *The Unbreakable Kimmy Schmidt*.

It turned out to be a great choice, but we hit a snafu after we finished season one: time. Life shifted and the little bits of time we'd been able to steal together for our binge-watching became harder and harder to find. The problem was mainly me.

Sophie begged me to let her watch season two of *Kimmy* by herself, as she had more time on her hands than I did. I told her no because I hadn't seen season two yet and I didn't know what kind of situations she'd be exposed to. I kept up my protective mom routine for a few weeks until I realized she'd already seen and heard plenty just by watching *The Office*. The problem wasn't the content. The problem again was me; I didn't want her to move on without me. Without a TV show to share, when would we hang out together?

Though I had my own personal milestones, like sharing a favorite sitcom with my daughter, she had goals of her own, like watching a TV show all by herself that wasn't written for kids. That was a rite of passage she needed. And I was holding her back.

So I relented and let her carry on with *Kimmy*. Without me.

It was fine. We could still trade jokes and references from *The Office* to make each other laugh, but it wasn't quite the same. When she was nearly at the end of the series, time shifted again. I was available, but too far behind for us to watch *Kimmy* together. So I started to watch the rest of the series on my own.

I created more time for myself by watching on the iPad with headphones so I could still be somewhat present for my younger daughter. I stayed up later than I should to squeeze in just one more episode. While my girls were doing schoolwork, I was watching *Kimmy* and laughing out loud, thus interrupting their focus. My LOLs made Sophie curious: Which episode was I on? What part was it? How many more episodes did I have left?

Again, it wasn't the same, but we were able to make silly *Kimmy* references to get each other to laugh. She started to cheer me on to make sure I got through the series as fast as I could. And then, the inevitable last episode arrived. I shared my tears with her and she laughed at me, but she understood.

Though we weren't able to watch all the episodes together, it still felt like a shared experience. We were also sharing a sense of humor no one in our house really "gets" but us. With that in mind, the next time she asked I let her watch *Parks and Rec* all by herself.

One day, not long after she'd finished *Parks and Rec*, Sophie made an offhand comment about one of the characters from the show and I responded with my own comment. My younger daughter was with us at the time and stated that she didn't get what we were talking about, so Sophie tried to explain it to her. Her sister still didn't really understand but they both just shrugged it off.

After a moment of thought, Sophie said to me, "We should find another show to watch."

I hope the humor and humanity of *The Office* made an impact on her, but mostly I hope she's never too cool to hang out with her mom. I don't know how easy it will be to find the time again to enjoy a show together, but I certainly didn't want to jinx her request by seeming too eager to make it work. At that moment I became hyper-aware I might put a hex of some sort on our plans if I didn't play it right, so I tried to keep my response low-key: "Yeah, sure. We can do that. If you want to."

I mean, to quote Michael Scott, I'm not superstitious...but I am a little stitious.

CANDY MICKELS MEJIA is a writer and mom based in suburban Houston. She writes about parenting, midlife, and mental health. You can read more of her work on her blog, *Slightly Overcaffeinated*, or find her on Twitter @cmickelsmejia.

18

THE LETTING GO

BY GRETCHEN KELLY

I have these lies I tell my kids over the years. I once told my son that Will Ferrell was the drummer for Red Hot Chili Peppers. "Elf is a rock star?" he asked in confusion as I swallowed my evil mom laugh.

"Yep. Weird, right?"

I throw out outrageous stories of my "past" to keep them guessing. My favorite lie is that I was a pop star in Europe before I met their dad. I sigh heavily, lamenting how I gave up fame and a career to get married and have kids. The real joy in this lie is that I'm a horrible singer. Like, *my babies would cry when I sang to them* bad. It's genius because it's so outrageous that they almost believe me. "Go ahead, ask your Grandma. She'll tell you," I say mysteriously and walk away, leaving them confused.

Silly jokes aside, I have a very honest parenting style. I don't shield or shelter them from much. I'm an open book. There are no secrets or illusions between my kids and me. Flaws on display, mistakes admitted, my own teen shenanigans are used as a lesson of how to be smarter than their mom. We are a very open family and no topic is off limits.

But there is one part of this parenting gig that I hide from them.

The part that has me catching my breath in fear and loss. The part I can't burden them with.

The letting go.

No one prepares you for this part. There is no "What To Expect When They Grow Up and Leave" that you can highlight and dog-ear until you feel armed with a road map. This is what we spend eighteen years prepping for. This is the goal: for them to be ready and capable of managing life without us. Whether it's college or the military or a job, it's the first step into adulthood and away from our watchful eye that is the kick in the stomach.

And oh, how that kick takes your breath away.

The night before we moved my oldest into his freshman dorm, we took him to a Jack White concert. It was not lost on me that his first concert was The Jonas Brothers when he was 10, how we graduated from screaming teens to a gritty rock show in eight years. How he had changed in those years. There were times during his high school days that he would come downstairs and my husband and I would be taken with the transformation in him from when he went up to his room. In the space of an hour he came down looking taller, voice deeper, his eyes more serious. He went from a silly preteen to an "almost man" overnight. But this night, his last night before college, was our send off. It was a celebration of his new life waiting for him. It was to share with him one of our favorite things, seeing live music. It was brilliant really. We were too busy having fun and collapsing in exhaustion when we got home to be sad about the next day.

Move in day was seamless. Met the roommates. Helped him get unpacked, bought a few last-minute necessities. He was excited. We were excited. He was getting ready to have the best years of his life. I wistfully thought back to my college freshman move-in day—and realized that we needed to leave. No one wants to kick their parents out on move-in day, but no one wants them lingering either.

"We should get going." As soon as the words left my mouth I felt betrayed by them. I needed to leave immediately before the tears overwhelmed me, but I didn't know if I could leave him. *How do you leave? How does this work?* I thought I was prepared. I'd had my emotional moments throughout his senior year. I choked up at his last swim meet, cried at graduation. *I already did the sad thing* I thought with gritted teeth.

We managed to hug goodbye and take pictures with strained smiles of parents who were pretending that their hearts weren't breaking. I didn't even make it to the parking garage before I collapsed in my husband's arms. We were both wracked with emotion. Our baby boy, the one who taught us how to be parents, was grown up. The boy who we marveled over in the way first-time parents are allowed to didn't need us anymore. Not the way he did before. He was the oldest of three, the son that was fiercely independent but still connected to us at every stage of growing up. The tenacious spirit that took on challenges of his own making just to prove he could do it. The sweet boy who would curl up to nap next to his dad on the couch. The boy who doted on his younger sisters and only mildly teased them because every oldest sibling gets some latitude with teasing.

The boy whose smile could light up a room. Who was passionate about his latest obsession, whether it was trucks or dinosaurs or skateboarding or music. Who would tell me everything, every thought. Who would ask me about things bigger than his young world, who wanted to travel the world and soak up every bit of life— he was grown up.

We drove home, alternating between silence and tearful memories and fears for how the next part would go. I laughed while wiping away the tears that wouldn't stop. "It's silly, right? We're being so overdramatic, right?"

No. We were grieving.

I know grief. My brother died of cancer when he was 18 years old. He never got a college send off. He never got to live in a dorm. Or experience the world as an adult. My parents experienced the worst kind of empty nest. I have lived with bone-crushing grief of losing my baby brother for twenty years now. And this, dropping my first born off at college, felt like grief. Not the same, but familiar.

· · ·

GRIEF ISN'T a straight line and it's not a monolithic experience. It comes in all forms and for different reasons. And this was a type of grief. It was a mourning of change. Of my changing role. It was tinged with joy and pride and excitement, but still grief. And I was prepared for none of it.

It's spending eighteen years parenting by instinct, then denying your instinct to hold them close when it's time for them to go. It feels unnatural. It is abrupt and jarring. Being a witness to your child growing up is to watch something spectacular that only parents and caretakers can truly understand. You hang on every development, every milestone, worry over every misstep and act of rebellion. You walk a tightrope between hovering and giving them too much freedom. You imagine every bad scenario and try to protect them while also letting them learn form their own mistakes. It's constant calibration.

And then one day, you're just...off duty. You're supposed to turn off that mode like a switch. You pace like a workhorse who doesn't know what a day off is. You wander the house in a fog, not sure how to fill the time, avoiding their empty room, all the while chastising yourself for the grief you're feeling. Feeling guilty for grief over something that is not tragic. What I know now is this is normal. If life was less cruel, it would be a slow dimming of the parenting "on switch"—but since when has life been gentle? Jump into the cold pool. Rip the band-aid off. That's how it goes. Eventually you find a new normal. A parenting from a distance, a way to be a sounding board and beacon when he needs it, but letting him go. Eventually you'll realize he's ok. He's thriving. He's grown up more than you could have imagined and your pride for this human you raised is overwhelming.

But that first phone call after he's left, that is the moment. The moment I started breathing easier. He was too busy to call or text much the first few weeks. I tortured myself with worry. *Was he struggling with homesickness? Was he so grateful to be away from us that he doesn't want to call? Was he partying too much?* These thoughts circled through my mind for two weeks. I didn't want him to know how hard this was on us. How quiet the house sounded with only two kids instead of three. How unnatural it felt to not see his face every day. This wasn't his burden to carry. It was ours. It was the cost of parenting and loving your child with everything you have. Missing him fiercely but not wanting him to know.

My phone rang.

"Hi, Mom."

I choke back tears. I'm happy for him. He's exactly where he's supposed to be.

"Mom, you ok?" Maybe he heard my heart breaking over the phone? I take a deep breath to steady my voice, "Yes, honey. I'm great."

Yeah. And I'm a former pop star too.

~

GRETCHEN KELLY IS A WRITER, activist, and mom of three. Social justice is the main driver of her writing. In addition to feminism and politics, she writes about grief, parenting, and random musings on life. She has appeared in *Upworthy, Huffington Post, Scary Mommy, Your Tango,* and was a featured writer and co-host of the *Stop Sexism* podcast for the Good Men Project. Follow @gkelly73 on Twitter.

19

MOTHER'S DAY

BY ANDREA CONTRERAS

O n Mother's Day, I call the woman who gave birth to my eldest son. Sometimes I text. I wish her happy Mother's Day and tell her I hope she is doing well. We catch up a bit. Wyatt and I used to call her together, but he is nearly 20 now, so he calls her on his own.

That's how long I've known Amy. Twenty years. She was a teenager when we first met, and I was a 32-year-old woman desperate for a child.

We have an open adoption, set up through an agency dedicated to establishing long-lasting ties between birth and adoptive parents. They believe this is healthier for the child, and I agree. The theory is my son is better served by knowing his birth parents, rather than by shrouding the particulars of the adoption in secrecy.

The agency pitches prospective adoptive parents with a fairy tale situation. It encourages birth parents and adoptive parents to create new traditions and celebrations around the child. I heard magical stories of how people built new families together with shared activities and camping trips. I met birth parents and adoptive parents who gushed about their close relationships. I wanted this too.

The agency suggested we come up with some kind of ritual for the day Amy relinquished Wyatt to us. I tried to involve my husband, but rituals were not really his thing. I was too embarrassed and ashamed to ask Amy what she might want to do. Wyatt's birth father was not in the picture at the time. So, I bought her a necklace—gold, with a locket. I have no idea if she still has it.

In the weeks I had spent getting to know her, I learned her big blue eyes and sweet, easy smile belied a steely resolve. Despite incredible pressure, she would not be deterred from doing what she believed was right for her and her child. Her own mother, who had Amy at an incredibly young age, mounted a campaign for her to keep Wyatt. For several weeks, Amy breastfed Wyatt and acted as though she might raise him while secretly contacting the adoption agency. Amy's mother was in no condition to help her and Amy had no one else.

The day we brought my son home was a typical winter day in the godforsaken weather of the Pacific Northwest. Gray, cold, raining. Baby Wyatt slept in his car carrier on the coffee table in the agency's office. Amy sat on the couch opposite me and my husband. She left him there while she went into the other room to sign papers. Then we did the same and it was time to go. I tried to say a few meaningful words, but the fact that the best day of our lives might be the worst day of hers overwhelmed me. I began to tear up and Amy looked at me sharply—a look I interpreted to mean "Don't you dare." So I didn't. It was the least I could do. On the way home, Wyatt started screaming. It took us a while to figure out he was hungry.

We did not become the smiling open adoption family on the agency's pamphlet. We did not set up special traditions or rituals. We did not go camping together. Every other month for a couple of years, Amy came to our house for Sunday lunch and to visit with Wyatt. Sometimes her brothers came and Wyatt played with them. Sometimes her mother, who eventually accepted the adoption, joined us. I stressed over providing enough food and whether I was making the right memories. Amy was relaxed and happy to see Wyatt. The last time we had one of these get-togethers, I was pregnant with my second child. I was so tired, I just threw some food together and eased myself into a chair while Wyatt played with his uncles. It was the best visit we ever had.

We moved out of state. Amy struggled finding jobs and housing while she tried to distance herself from her difficult beginnings. I divorced my husband and felt I had let her down; she placed her child in my care and now I was breaking up his home.

We kept in touch, of course. Even though she was transient at times, she always made sure I had her phone number. And then Facebook came along, and we could be involved with each other more easily. I remarried. Amy also met someone and settled down.

Wyatt grew old enough to have a phone and I saved Amy's number in it. He called her on his own more often. To my great embarrassment, he asked her for money for his birthday one year and she sent it. I wanted to call her and ask her not to do that, or tell her she did not need to feel manipulated, but what business was it of mine, really? What I wanted, I realized, was to let her know I was not the sort of mother who thought his request was okay. I wanted her to think I was doing a good job. I think she still sends him money on his birthday.

When Wyatt was a child, I believed how he turned out was up to me. I believed I bore the responsibility for him to become a well-rounded, healthy human being. His father and I provided music lessons and enrolled him in sports. Summers were filled with camps focusing on art, skateboarding, and even farming. If he expressed an interest, we were on it. I wanted to open up his head and pour everything he might need into it.

When Wyatt reached puberty, he was suddenly full of rage and willpower. As a child, he had been high energy. It was difficult to get him to sit still, but he was a happy kid. Not anymore. He hated my new husband. He hated school. He hated his father. I couldn't make him go to school. I couldn't make him stay in the house—let alone in his room—at night. I couldn't make him do anything. We took him to no less than three different therapists. I went to a therapist. We went to therapy together. We sent him to a military academy thinking the structure would help. Later, when he got expelled, Amy was the first one he called.

We sent him to wilderness boot camp and therapeutic boarding school. He loved both, but for two years, I lugged around the shame of not being a better mother. I always let Amy know what we were doing, assuring her he was safe. I told her we thought this would help him. The truth was I wanted her to absolve the terrible guilt I carried; she entrusted her child to me, and I sent him away. I wondered if he would have been better off with her. *Would she have more patience? Would she know to do something I did not?*

Wyatt came home to stay at the beginning of his junior year in high school. He was not deeply damaged, as I feared. Instead, he seemed to have settled into himself. He had started playing guitar again and could build a fire out of nothing. Taller than I was now, he would put his arm around my shoulders and tell me to chill out. When he made a joke I didn't approve of, he nudged me and said, "Oh come on, that was funny!" So I let him make me laugh.

I tried letting go of my idea of what motherhood should look like and started accepting both of us as we are. It was almost too late, but I stopped making Wyatt's development about me. I tried to observe him instead. I noticed how he took most of life in stride, very much like Amy. I noticed he still had a steely will, very much like Amy. I also heard him say words of advice and comfort to others I knew I'd said to him in the past. I slowly realized motherhood is not so much a task to perfect as it is a process of letting go.

When Amy got married, I sent Wyatt on a plane to be there. He was 18 and they had not seen each other since he was small. He went fishing with the uncles he did not remember. He hung out with Amy's new husband. Amy texted me a picture of herself in a wedding dress, standing on her porch with Wyatt. In the picture, the two of them are grinning with the same blue eyes.

Not long ago, Wyatt and his wolf pack of friends were eating pizza in my living room. They were scheming about how to pull off some get-rich-quick ventures: video game design or maybe real estate development. I had no idea how they came up with the idea of investing in apartment buildings. I had no idea where they were planning to find the money. I had some ideas and opinions, but I just listened. Wyatt said they should invest in property in the state where he was born. It was less expensive, he said, and "I have family there."

We are not what I imagined the smiling family on the adoption agency's pamphlet was all about. We will never have traditions or rituals. We will never go camping together. I doubt that family really exists anyway. Instead, we cobbled together something else. Like a reverse Jenga game, we placed our blocks tentatively on top of each other. Some of them fell off and we had to replace them. Some of them are sticking out and don't look very pretty; but this is our family.

These days, I occasionally ask Wyatt if he has spoken with Amy. I have shepherded his relationship with her, but now they can make it as they wish. He says they Snapchat. I still call her on Mother's Day.

ANDREA CONTRERAS IS a lawyer by day and writer whenever else she can squeeze it in. Her flash fiction has been published in a small local paper that went out of business. She lives in Southern California with two dogs, a cat, and two teenaged boys who are only grumpy 60 percent of the time.

20

A HARD "C"

BY SARA WEBER

My mom and older sister used to argue. A lot. Not little spats but all-out, red-faced scream-fests.

No matter what they were fighting about, inevitably my mom would spit out her closer: "I hope you have a child JUST LIKE YOU."

It wasn't meant as an encouragement. My sister was mouthy, loved to talk back, and thought she knew everything. Eventually, my mom got her wish. My sister did end up having a kid just like her. But, oddly enough, so did I.

Perhaps I would have been a mouthy kid if I had been firstborn. But I was third and last, the baby and peacemaker. I was the joker who tried to diffuse every domestic battle between my siblings, parents and siblings, or parents themselves—but being cute and funny only went so far. I knew my place because my older siblings often reminded me of it. When my siblings moved out to go to college, I thought my peacemaking work was done. I would often turn to my parents and say "See? This is the way it was supposed to be. Easy."

And then came Chloe.

When my daughter was born, she came out screaming. She

almost seemed pissed off, like "Wow, that sure took long enough, didn't it?" It was almost as if I was a grave and lasting disappointment to her already. The tension was already there: little did she appreciate how the "pushing part" of labor nearly did me in. It made me finally decide that I didn't care if my spleen, kidneys, and stomach all fell out with this kid, I needed her out. Period.

No cooing afterglow, she burst from the womb pronouncing her personality on an unsuspecting world. Wrinkly, pink, covered in gunk and screaming her head off. Her father and I had intended on calling her "Lael Klasiena." But when she came out giving us a piece of her mind, we knew she was a kid with a hard C in her name. A big... Chloe.

She wouldn't nurse, no matter how much I begged and pleaded. As a toddler, every question was followed by "NO! Me do it!" (If she was in a good mood, she'd just look at me sympathetically and say "Noie, Noie, Chloe do it"—a poet from day one). But, along with the stubbornness, came a ferocious loyalty that was like no other. When Chloe was 2, I was sitting on a friend's deck while a group of our kids played in the yard. There was a commotion, and when I looked, one toddler was trying to impose his will on another. Chloe would have none of it. She got up in front of the little guy with her hands on her hips, just giving it to the 2-year-old bruiser. Of course, she was spouting gibberish, but we knew what she was saying: "Mess with my friend, mess with me."

It can be trying to raise a spitfire when you have a partner, when you can kind of spell each other off, but it is a whole different ball game when you are raising one solo. When Chloe's dad and I parted ways, Chloe took it hard. She would sit on the steps of my "new to us" townhouse and weep over missing her dad. When I'd try to hold her, she would shake me off. Chloe was 8, and of course, couldn't understand why the people who were most important to her couldn't live together.

Fast forward to 2020. My beautiful, strong-willed kid is now 15 and a half, 5'11", and she got the best and the absolute worst of me. When we are good, we are really, really good. She is funny, kind, interesting, and aware of the world around her. But when she is stressed about anything (work, a friend situation, Tuesday), she will take it out on me. She will look at the smallest thing and snap at it. A few weeks ago, we were watching a baking competition show, and I said something about the editing of the show and how it kind of gave away the winner. She screamed, "It's like you are attacking me over this show, it's NOT MY FAULT." And stormed off to her bedroom.

We had a bad stretch after Christmas. Maybe it was splitting up the holidays, maybe it was the January blahs, but she was on the attack all day, every day. I'd ask her to get off screens. Her response: "No." I'd ask her to go to bed on time. Her response: blank stare. I'd ask her to stop eating so much junk. Her response: eye roll. And I was worn out.

Now, usually, I would go to my ol' standby, handed down from generation to generation: the "screaming my head off about everything that had gone bad in the last three years and blaming everyone but myself" method. But I was tired. So I decided to try something different.

I said "Chloe, I struggle with anxiety and some other mental health issues, one being that I'm a recovering addict. So when I see you on your phone all day or eating obsessively, I feel like you may be heading down the same destructive path I did. And I get worried." I didn't say it that eloquently or calmly. I said it in wheezy breaths between sobs. She looked stunned. Her first question? "What are you addicted to?" I wanted to say, "Well, that depends on what time in my life we're talking." But what I did say was "I'm not ready to talk about it yet, but maybe I'll tell you when you're 18." Oh shit.

I had been thinking about getting a tattoo for years and decided to get one last January, on the occasion of my forty-fifth birthday. It was simple, just the word "Forgive (n)," to remind me to forgive myself, to forgive others, and that I am forgiven. I was going to make the tattoo a big occasion. My sister and her daughter came up from Buffalo for it, and Chloe was going to go with me. The four of us would go out for Mexican food after. Knowing a lot about the art of tattooing, I explained my elaborate plans of who would sit with me through the long process. I told the artist, "Chloe will be in here for the first part and then my sister, then my niece and then Chloe again." The artist said, "Um, yeah, this is going to take less than five minutes." Oh, okay.

So my plan was revised where for sure Chloe would be there for the beginning and the end and my sister and niece would sneak in during the middle. The first two letters went fine and it was super fun to sit there with my daughter. Then it got a wee bit painful. When Chloe came back in and the artist, Kim, finished the lettering with an "All done," I looked at the tattoo and it was more beautiful than I could have imagined. Then I looked at Chloe and burst into tears. She just smiled. Forgive (n).

I know I'm not always going to succeed in talking calmly and neither will she. And she will continue to attack me when something else is worrying her. But something changed for me at that moment. If we continue to attempt to forgive each other and remind ourselves that we are forgiven, then things may be okay. If we remember that "Hurt people hurt people" and stop slinging blame at each other, then we may be able to soften. If we swallow our pride daily, even by the minute, and ask for forgiveness, we may survive these years of hormones and worry. And if all else fails, I can just move to Antarctica the day before her eighteenth birthday.

SARA WEBER IS an actor and playwright from Huntsville, Alabama. Because her dream of writing and performing on SNL has not panned out, Sara has enjoyed performing her one-woman shows in church basements and community centers all over Canada and the USA. She currently resides in Hamilton, Ontario with her two kids and rescue hound, Karl. Learn more at saraweber.ca.

21

T.G.I.F.

BY GILA PFEFFER

When I was a kid in the 80s, one of my favorite shows was *Out of This World*. Perhaps you remember it. The main character, Evie, lives with her mother and communicates with her absent alien father through a crystal cube. I now realize how stupid that plotline is, but I was 12 years old at the time and we didn't have cable. Because Evie is half alien, she possesses a superpower: By touching the points of her fingers together she can freeze time.

Back then, given the choice to have any one superpower myself, that's the one I'd have chosen. I imagined being able to stay up as late as I wanted, raid the snack cabinet without my mother lecturing me about healthy eating, and give myself some extra time to finish a school assignment. But younger me was on to something because given that same option as the mother of four teens that I am today, I'd still opt for the ability to make time stand still, even if only for a minute to catch my breath.

When my kids were little and I was in the trenches, so to speak, the days passed by slowly. My children needed a lot of time and attention which I was usually happy to give. But by 5:00 p.m. each day I'd be staring at the kitchen clock, willing it to tick faster toward bedtime. I'd traded a career in fashion marketing for one as a stay-at-home mom, and while I wore that title with great honor, I also accepted that this was my new job. And not everyone loves every part of their job.

It was when my oldest went off to middle school that I first noticed time speeding up. And because my kids are all two years or less apart, it wasn't long before they'd all left the cozy predictability of elementary school, their standard issue smart phones in hand. Suddenly they had more homework, more extracurricular activities, and more friends from different neighborhoods. Social media meant that their network now extended well beyond our family, so I spent more time in the car shuttling them around. It also meant more of my time and energy spent monitoring their phone use, an ongoing battle even today. They were busy and I was busy trying to support their often-overlapping schedules while managing our household and processing the barrage of emails that poured in from school and parent chat groups every day. Times four.

There are never enough hours in the day to get through my to-do list and I know that the problem is exacerbated in a world where our attention is the number one commodity to companies vying for our business. Screens demand our attention for every aspect of our lives from working to shopping to communicating to wellness. I struggle with the paradox that the apps we are encouraged to use for head space and sleep are on the very devices that rob us of both.

There are many ways families can create more space for better parent-teen communication and more family time in general. One option is a good, old-fashioned pandemic that forces all of you to be in close quarters indefinitely. Of course, there are other strategies.

While freezing time is still the stuff of fiction, my family and I are able to slow it down once a week by carrying on a tradition that has been passed down on both sides of the family tree for thousands of years. We observe the Sabbath.

The ways in which people observe the Sabbath, or "Shabbat" as we call it, vary depending on one's own family traditions, but essentially it is a time to take a break from the week to rest, introspect, and strengthen connections with family and friends for a twenty-four hour period beginning every Friday evening at sundown. Just as a sabbatical is a period of paid leave given to university professionals after seven years of work, Shabbat offers a respite from the demands of the world every seventh day of the week. It's the embodiment of T.G.I.F.

Continuing the traditions we practiced in our respective childhood homes, my husband and I sit down with our four children each Friday night to enjoy some traditional foods like challah bread and homemade chicken soup as well as some more modern cuisine. And wine. Always wine. Because teens.

When they were little, the kids would use this time to share some projects they'd made or a song they'd learned in school. The use of any electronic items is prohibited during Shabbat so there was no TV after dinner. These were the days before smart phones and streaming services, so going off the grid was easier. After dinner the kids would play a bit and get to bed, leaving my husband and I to debrief each other on the week's news from our various fronts. Or just pass out on the couch like the exhausted parents we were.

The older my kids got, the more I looked forward to hitting the pause button each week and having some meaningful interactions with them. School, work, and community demands only increased as the years passed, and by the time they were all in the double digits, they had iPhones, which further consumed their attention. Finding uninterrupted time to talk without the constant dinging of our phones can be challenging.

As impossible as it may sound in our tech-fueled world, we switch off all of our devices at the beginning of Shabbat and leave them that way for twenty-four hours. I once heard someone use the term "disconnecting to connect" and I think that's an accurate description of what we do. Our ability to put the harried week aside and really talk to, sometimes at, each other is aided by the fact that there is zero chance that any of us will be interrupted by an email, notification, phone call or other activity. Talking over a family dinner IS the activity. And the older they get, the more important and the trickier it is to get them talking.

One tradition my family adopted recently is that we each list something about the past week that made us happy, something that upset us, and something we are looking forward to in the near future. We refer to this as "Rose, Thorn, Bud," inspired by a friend of ours who told us about his own family Friday night practice. At first not everyone was on board with this. Certain family members thought it was corny. But over time even they have come to appreciate the cathartic benefits of reviewing the highs and lows of the week in a safe and supportive space.

In case you're picturing an idyllic scene out of a movie where everyone at the table extends mutual respect without any sarcastic swipes, allow me to divest you of that illusion. My kids are 19, 17, 15, and 13; their sibling rivalry is alive and well. All it takes is one thrown barb and Word War III ensues. Sometimes someone storms away from the table. Sometimes that someone is me. But more often than not, this doesn't happen until after we've had some robust family dialogue about the events of the week, from personal encounters to world news.

Separating to connect is something that the coronavirus lock-downs have brought into sharp focus. As many people sheltered in place, they found themselves with more time on their hands for self-reflection and a realignment of values and priorities. In the early days, I heard some people refer to it as pressing the reset button on life. Of course, now we know that lockdown lasted far longer than we could have imagined it would and the "New pandemic, new me!" sentiments gave way to stress and aggravation. But the early days, the ones when it felt like we'd just called for a short timeout, are what remind me so much of Shabbat's core meaning.

You may be wondering what the value of Shabbat is during a pandemic when our family is home, together, ALL THE TIME for months on end. For us it has served several functions, the most basic of which is to mark the days of the week. Frankly the only one that had been in any way distinguishable as the days and weeks bled into each other was Saturday. Separating from our screens proved to be very helpful in our attempts to get a break from the relentless news cycle and social media. As nearly every aspect of life was reduced to pixels, the weekly break was a welcome one. Furthermore, all of my kids were perpetually zoned off into their individual worlds (i.e. their bedrooms) of schoolwork, Netflix, and Snapchat, so by the time Friday night rolled around we were indeed ready for another chance to share our thoughts on what was going on in the world. It will come as no surprise to you that for many weeks, everyone's "thorn" (the worst part of the week) was being stuck at home without their friends.

When things feel unstable, our instinct is to seek out the familiar and the reliable, sort of like when we reach for comfort food in times of stress. Shabbat is hardwired into our way of life and it is non-transferable. We can't decide to observe it on a Tuesday, for instance. It is there, ever dependable, waiting for us at the end of each week. Coronavirus has cancelled many things that my kids were looking forward to—concerts, travel plans, a bar mitzva—but Shabbat is immune to the effects of the virus. It must be my chicken soup.

GILA PFEFFER IS an American freelance writer, blogger, and mother raising four teens in the UK. She draws on her experience as a parent to connect with her audience through her poignant, relatable content. As a breast cancer pre-vivor and survivor, she is a staunch prevention advocate who gives talks and writes in the breast cancer space as well. You can find Gila on her social media platforms here: @gilapfeffer.

22

UNTANGLED

BY SANTORINA DAVIS

In the summer of 2001, I was newly 19 years old, belly swollen with an illegitimate child, filling a prophecy in a line of single unwed mothers. The day my son was born I toddled into the labor and delivery ward with my mother on my arm, prepared for the passing of the parental torch without ever pausing to be just a woman. My sky-blue cotton pajama pants were covered in rainbows with puffy clouds on the tips. I had three metal rings in my lower lip and one glinting in my eyebrow. My water broke at home in a trickle, then a gush, the intensity of his impending arrival a slow burn echoing the build of love and acceptance I'd felt in the early stages of the pregnancy. I had a hand towel tucked into my panties to catch the flow of amniotic fluid and the nurse took one look at me and wondered if I hadn't just peed my pants. The uncertainty and distrust of my parenting started right then, with one foot still in the elevator.

My son broke into this world and claimed me as his own, my hospital gown caught in the ball of his tiny fist after I dragged him the length of my body to where I could kiss his slick, misshapen newborn head. I had no idea in that moment the ways I would lose myself in him.

It was easy to imagine the endless screaming and refusal to sleep was an infant phase. And in preschool, when the teachers insisted they needed more help supervising his intense agitation, the doctors I consulted would wave their hands, convinced he would outgrow it, that possibly I just had no idea how to do this mothering thing. When my son's intensity magnified in kindergarten, I quit my college classes, then my job, to focus on advocating for him.

Over the years I would watch my son melt down in public places long after it was socially acceptable to lay on the ground and do so, trying to use my own body to make his display invisible to shocked and judgmental onlookers. He would scream for hours about imaginary cracks in his clothing, so I sought out clothes with no seams or tags and learned to put his socks on just right. He would punch holes into walls and chase me into a bathroom, his infant siblings in my arms, while he beat the door with a baseball bat. He would exhaust himself on his rage and tuck himself back into me, eyes filled with tears and confusion while he wondered aloud why he was the way he was. I had no answers for him, only a deep hope that I could love him enough to fix this and a nagging belief that I could not.

As he grew older and his desperation and sadness reached dangerous proportions, I would sit next to him in hospital rooms, holding his hand while he cried through the haze of sedatives. I would sign paperwork to send him to facilities I prayed would "fix" him since I had not yet been enough to do so.

Waves of diagnoses and social-service referrals crashed upon us, leading to endless hours of IEP meetings and shuttling to therapists and doctors who often shrugged their shoulders but looked back at me as the cause and culprit of his indiscretions.

There would be years where I would bring him home to teach and then try, ever hopeful, to integrate him back into special education classrooms. These classrooms, created in the name of safety, offered little more than social isolation, so I would offer myself up as a playmate and confidante when no others existed in his world. When he should have been pulling away to find his own way, we found ourselves tangled even tighter.

Then, in his junior year of high school, he was the target of false accusations that led to an FBI investigation. I pulled him out of school one final time to teach him until he graduated from our home-based classroom, senior class of one.

Raising this boy consumed me in every sense of the word, on every level, for the entirety of my adult life. Because the world seemed so jagged and sharp against him, over the years I slowly molded myself into a protective shield around him. As I grew into an adult alongside him, I began to imagine we moved through the world as one entity; when he would ebb away from me I would reach out and try to pull him back to where it was safe, where I could dole out the harshness of the world in bite-sized pieces. As he became a young man, this pulling away felt violent and personal to me, my attempts to hold him close and safe more desperate. By the time I found myself standing on the cusp of his transition to adulthood, I did not know how to let him go. I wasn't sure he was ready to face the world alone but more than that, I wasn't sure who I was without him.

On the eve of my son's eighteenth birthday, we stood in the kitchen, surrounded by friends who had known us his entire life. With one minute to midnight, I wrapped my arms around him, his body stretched six inches taller than my own. He balked and pulled away, but I held tight and whispered "Just lean into it. I want to be holding you as you turn 18."

The minute hand ticked over. The anticipation of that moment had been building to a fever pitch for the past year, and yet it felt no different than the one before. I reached up on the very tip of my toes and kissed his head, sang him "Happy Birthday" and then followed him upstairs, tucking him into bed for the first time in forever, one last time.

The next morning, I drove him to a business park to meet with a lawyer who explained how, in the days to come, we would file a petition with the courts to appoint him a legal guardian. A judge who'd never met him would decide, based upon stacks of doctors' reports and suggestions of people who'd met with him in one-hour increments, if he was capable of making sound decisions regarding his own care.

Had I done enough? Had I done too much? In the years since I had toddled into the labor and delivery ward, I'd worked so hard to slowly untangle my limbs from my own mother that I hadn't realized how tightly I'd wound them around my son. In an attempt to shield him from the world, I had robbed him of the autonomy needed to experience the world at full throttle. They say "Babies don't keep" but there I was, with a son who was now an adult and I'd kept him far longer than most.

I knew in my heart that filing the petition was the right thing to do. As much as my little boy's body had grown into a man's, his mind hadn't quite caught up. Regular teenage mood swings were heightened with periods of severe mania, juxtaposed with weeks of barely being able to get out of bed. I hoped it wouldn't always be this way for him. I hoped he'd continue to grow and understand, to learn to advocate for himself in the years to come. I hoped there would be a point when he'd remember to swallow the little pills that helped keep him stable on his own. I hoped that someday, despite all odds, he would get the best of his disease and come out on the other side, stronger and greater for the tests it put upon him.

A few weeks into his life as a legal adult, I sat behind my son in the courtroom and watched the steely set of his shoulders as the judge looked and spoke directly to him and delivered the news: He was being deemed incompetent to care for himself. A third-party legal guardian was assigned, and we would convene again at his twenty-first birthday to reassess the need to continue with legal guardianship.

We all knew this was coming and yet hearing the words from the mouth of this stranger in the black robes felt so harsh. My son nodded and then rose to leave, brushed past me without looking me in the eye and moved ever so slightly out of my reach as I put my hand out to console him. He did not want me to tell him it would be okay. He did not want me to try to explain again in ways that might make better sense why this was necessary.

That night I snuck into his room and whispered words of love and affirmation into his ear as he slept. I brushed his thick hair off his broadened face and wished that I could turn back time, do it all over once more with the hindsight gained from struggling against the world together all those years.

I am proud of the way my son continues to work toward the best version of himself. I'm proud of how fiercely he loves his family and his friends, how giving of himself he can be when someone in his life really needs it. Despite the years of struggles he's faced, he's somehow managed to retain a sense of childlike wonder at the world, a trust that most people are good deep down inside. I hope he never loses that.

I am proud, too, of the way I'm learning to unfold myself from him, slow and painful as it may be. My eyes are adjusting to see his face as his own finally, not as an extension of mine or a reflection of the man who helped me make him. The tiny baby I drug up the length of my body on the day he was born has now drug me through the length of his childhood. His fist no longer twists around the neck of my hospital gown. Now, the tips of his fingers barely graze my own as he towers next to me. He says it less often and in ways that are harder to hear, but even as he pulls away to become his own man I can hear the echo: You are mine. Forever and ever.

That need whirls around me with familiar temptation. I may never know if the decisions I've made were the right ones, if the ways I navigated us through this world were to his detriment. My son will always need me. But I am finally sure enough to step both feet off the elevator and into the newfound confidence that we will both be alright on our own.

~

SANTORINA DAVIS IS the author of the blog *No, But Really...*, and has been a featured performer at the sold out show *The Mamalogues*. Santorina Davis is a Northern California native who now proudly resides in the Land of Enchantment with her husband, four children, and harem of domestic animals. When she's not busy clawing her way through motherhood she manages press relations for the family business.

23

NERDMASTE: THE DIVINE AWKWARD IN ME HONORS THE DIVINE AWKWARD IN YOU

BY NANEA HOFFMAN

I'm 12 years old, about to be 13, and I'm crying my eyes out in a bathroom stall thinking: *not fair not fair not fair.* I've just lost the election for student body president by sixteen votes. I sit in Sister Marie Celeste's office as the ballots are counted and listen to the news, my grin a rictus across my face.

I know that the word "rictus" means a kind of death grin, because I just read a book in which half the population of an imaginary country is wiped out by the plague and riddled with grinning corpses.

My opponent jumps up from her chair and hugs me excitedly. She's a cheery, cute cheerleader who already wears bras not from the training section. Her bras have a job to do while mine remain purely ceremonial. She has perfectly feathered bangs and has already kissed boys. I hate that she's being nice to me.

"Congratulations," I manage, keeping my voice even. Then I bolt before the tears start.

It's really dumb. I should be thrilled I got this far. That's what I tell myself, anyway, as I sit on the can in my sailor suit uniform, sniffling into a wad of toilet paper.

I am a nerd. A misfit. An outsider and not in the cool S.E. Hinton way. I had some nerve even running. I should have known it was a popularity contest, and that as the bookworm with *Battlestar Galactica* framed glasses and an annoyingly large vocabulary, I had very little chance. No one is impressed with my obsession with *Star Blazers* or the fact that I've read the entire *Little House on the Prairie* series four times. Not even my teachers. In one excruciatingly boring science class—something about measuring liquid in beakers—I have a fantasy novel hidden inside the school textbook that I've already read beginning to end. The teacher catches sight of my tattered copy of *Silver on the Tree* by Susan Cooper and rips it, enraged, from my startled hands. She hurls it across the room, roaring, "That's what I think of THAT!" I'm humiliated. The other girls laugh, exchanging knowing looks.

I hate that this is the way things are. Was this the moment I decided to run? Putting myself in the spotlight when I'm near the bottom of the pecking order in an all-girls Catholic school is like deciding to go for a swim in shark-infested waters.

I don't know where this stubborn belief comes from, but I think I might be able to win if I campaign on the ISSUES: better student events, playground mentors, baked-good fundraisers at recess. I foolishly believe the same forty girls I've been with since kindergarten will view me differently once they hear my ideas.

My campaign speech is eloquent and impassioned, but it can't hold a candle to the cheer my opponent's friends perform for her. It's set to the cadence of "Let's Get A Little Bit Rowdy" but they change the words to "Let's! Get! A little bit votes for Suzy Tanaka! Right! Now!" The egregious grammatical errors don't trouble the crowd the way they do me.

Unfazed, I plunge into the second part of my plan, a blitzkrieg of stickers distributed by my handful of geeky friends to the younger students. I'm aiming for the fickle but crucial kindergarten through third grade votes.

On week two of the campaign, I switch to scratch 'n sniff stickers, which cost more of my carefully hoarded allowance money but turn out to be a genius move. This is how I pull within sixteen votes of victory despite my bottle-thick glasses, unfashionably frizzy hair, and *Leave It to Beaver*-esque buck teeth.

Now, it's over, and I'm perched on a toilet seat in the white-tiled bathroom, with my scuffed-up Oxford shoes tucked up on the seat so I can hug my knees to my achy chest. I'm not crying so much because I lost, but because I'd been hoping against hope that through my campaigning, I'd have been accepted.

I'm hiccupping quietly in my stall when I hear two of the popular girls walk in. They've taken great pleasure over the years in making fun of me for the way I talk. In Hawaii, a kid who grows up not speaking Pidgin because her mother insists on proper English in the home is likely to get her ass beat for being "hybolic." As in "Eh, why you tryin' fo' ac'? How come you gotta talk all hybolic li'dat?" They ridicule my clothes. On free dress days, I wear a Member's Only jacket but it's obviously my dad's, and even when I roll up the sleeves, it hangs on me like curtains. They fundamentally do not get that I *like* reading *Little Women* at recess instead of rushing out to the ball court to play dodgeball—which in my book is adult-sanctioned, kid-on-kid violence.

"So, that Nanea kid actually tried to run for president?" asks Popular Girl #1. "I know," laughs Popular Girl #2. "It's like she forgot she's a nerd." I wait fifteen minutes after they leave before I emerge. I'm late to class, but the teacher loves me, so I don't get a demerit.

What I want to tell that angry little 12-year-old girl is, "Hold on! The age of the nerds is coming! All the things that make you different and strange are the things that people will LOVE you for someday." Twelve-year-old me doesn't know that someday a magical thing called the "internet" will exist and it will connect her to her fellow disenfranchised weirdos. She doesn't know that loving passionately, weirdly, unashamedly is a gift. She doesn't know that in the future, people will proudly claim the title of nerd and geek and fangirl. She only knows that right now the word is thrown like a stone.

In the gauntlet of middle school, all of my focus is on blending. I'm not the kind of nerd who doesn't care what people think. I care so much I have anxiety attacks over it (12-year-old me could have benefited from a generalized anxiety disorder diagnosis). I *want* to fit in, but I just don't have the social savvy. And I'm probably too cerebral for my own good. I like strange books and big words. I read the *Encyclopedia Britannica* for *fun,* for God's sake (again, c'mon *INTERNET,* hurry up). It's no wonder I love stories about space and far away kingdoms. Maybe in a different galaxy, far, far away, I'd be normal.

What happens is that I leave the tiny little school at age 14 for a bigger high school and the tiny little island in the middle of the Pacific—briefly for college, and then permanently after I get married. I take with me my anxiety and nerdish tendencies. I grow into myself. I stop being shy about showing my weird because: 1) No matter how strange or obsessive your love is, someone else out there shares it and is DYING to talk to you about it—and maybe write some fanfiction, too; and 2) How else can you find the right people if you don't wear your Hogwarts house affiliation or your Jayne hat openly?

What I learn is that I should never forget that I'm a nerd. I learn that most people have a bit of nerd in them as well, and that should be celebrated. I greet you, fellow weirdos. Nerdmaste. The divine awkward in me honors the divine awkward in you.

NANEA HOFFMAN IS the founder of *Sweatpants & Coffee.* She writes, makes things, and drinks an inordinate amount of coffee. She is also extremely fond of sweatpants. She believes in love, peace, joy, comfort, and caffeinated beverages.

24

SHAKE WHAT YOUR MAMA GAVE YA!

BY RACHEL SOBEL

I n my life, I have accomplished a lot. I have multiple degrees under my belt as well as a long and successful career that I eventually parlayed into my own business. I navigated a divorce with a toddler on my hip and blended a family by having a baby two weeks before I turned 40. I've even mastered the art of carrying a toddler in mid-meltdown under my arm like a football out of a crowded store. But when it came to having a tween, I found out I knew nothing at all. Not a damn thing. Not shit.

The heartfelt moments of motherhood are rivaled by so many humbling ones, like when you think you finally have it together and the next thing you know you are in the middle of the mall dealing with a diaper blowout and forgot to pack clean diapers, and wipes for that matter, in your overpriced diaper bag you thought was a necessity, and end up hoarding napkins from the mediocre Asian spot in the food court. But raising a tween is next level.

Because none of these things compare to how you feel when your own flesh and blood can cut you down with only a single eye roll.

My tween, my firstborn, is initiating my hazing into this sisterhood. Many of her habits are foreign to me, a feeling I'm sure is passed down from generations of mothers, all looking to remain relevant in their tweens' lives amid the bazillion distractions, mostly in the form of technology. My daughter and I are tight and have the whole open communication thing down, which is key since it's my job to infuse her mind with accurate information instead of the garbage she learns from other kids during recess. And in case you didn't know, recess puts the "cess" in cesspool. It's a breeding ground for fake news about EVERYTHING—sex, drugs, and the trash music coming out of TikTok. It's where kids congregate and share information with total conviction, creating the most ridiculous game of telephone ever. Which reminds me, many of you have not had the sex talk with your kids yet and it shows.

I actually think the whole TikTok movement is one of the most interesting pastimes of the tween species in this era. They are addicted and an informed parent can spot a TikToker anywhere in the wild. Don't know what I'm talking about? Everywhere you look there are tweens engaging in some sort of choreography, mostly involving wildly jerking arm movements mixed in with body rolls of varying degrees. Some innocent and some that make Cardi B look like a devout nun.

Once you have witnessed the phenomenon in your own home, you can't unsee it, and you'll begin to notice it all the damn time. The kid in the front passenger seat of the car next to you at the red light flailing his arms while his mom looks numb in the driver's seat. The kid trailing behind a parent in the grocery store coming dangerously close to knocking over cans of creamed corn while perfecting "the whoa" (that's seriously a name of a coveted move and my kid has the nerve to make fun of my generation for doing "the running man"). The kid in the waiting room of the pediatrician's office who spots another kid doing a similar routine but instead of acknowledging each other and maybe joining forces to perform a cool duet, they remain siloed while having a weird non-communicative dance off. It's always the same no matter the song. The arms fly up and down at warp speed. The hips might rock side to side. It almost mimics some sort of secret tween sign language. Maybe the joke is on us and they are all plotting to stage the biggest coup ever as they communicate in passing with one another. Parents of TikTok-ing tweens just look at each other and nod in solidarity. No words need to be spoken at all, kind of like the silent dance off.

I've learned that TikTok can also come in handy to bond with your tweens if you are willing to look like a moron until you get the hang of it and endure the palpable frustration emitting from your child as they try to teach you the latest dance challenge. This is where I feel like my generation and my tween's can collide and coexist. Because a huge part of TikTok is the dancing and I practically exited the womb straight into a dance class. I'm a step ahead of the game. I was born for this part of motherhood. From strapping up the first pair of ballet shoes at 3 years old, through countless dance recitals and competitions, my dance career culminated at the age of 18 when I shook my ass poolside in a bikini top and a pair of hoochie shorts on MTV for an eighteen-episode stint of a show called *The Grind*. My parents were shockingly not put off by me being MTV famous and thought it was bragworthy as hell. Even my grandmothers watched from their retirement community clubhouses following some cutthroat canasta to catch a glimpse of me gyrating and body rolling the day away. For anyone in my demographic, *The Grind* can be counted as a major accomplishment and instills a huge amount of street cred. To a tween however, it's cringeworthy and makes no sense since all they know about MTV is that there is no music showcased whatsoever. My coolness is fossilized right before my eyes with my daughter's blasé attitude about my dancing prowess. But she can't take away my rhythm.

So, in order to connect with her and spend quality time, I dusted off my hoodrat moves and learned the elusive art of TikTok dances. This, in her eyes, makes me cool and relatable. The music mostly sucks but I'll deal just to be with her in her element. She tells me I'm doing almost every move wrong. She huffs and puffs when I miss steps. But my God, when we nail a TikTok she smiles and the glare from her metal braces sparkles in the light of our makeshift living room dance studio. She looks at me like I'm Beyoncé, or maybe that's just what I see. She is not impressed that mama won her fair share of "booty dancing" competitions back in the day when old school hip hop ruled supreme. But she sure does love when we tackle a TikTok and are completely in sync.

I know she will only continue to grow as a young lady establishing her own independence and I'm all for it. I'm thankful for the hugs she still gives and may just hold on a little tighter and longer before she tells me I'm being weird. She doesn't need me for the little stuff anymore, like kissing boo-boos or squeezing just the right amount of toothpaste on her Hello Kitty toothbrush. But she does need me for bigger stuff. More adult stuff. And I will be there no matter how many times she tells me I'm annoying or singing the song lyrics wrong. As she evolves and finds her own way, I will only love her harder. I remember my own mom telling me that all the times you worry when your kids are babies—high fevers, developmental milestones, transitioning out of a car seat—all pale in comparison to when your kids become teens and start to find their own voices and ways.

I get it now.

I worry she'll be apprehensive to share certain things with me. I'm nervous for when she starts dating and experiences that heartbreak for the first time that feels paralyzing in the moment but laughable as an adult. I'm petrified for middle school and mean girls. Sometimes all of it seems overwhelming and all I can do is constantly tell her that I have her back through life, despite the 'tude she may throw my way. I will laugh with her, cry with her, love the shit out of her and even do the damn "whoa," if that's what she needs. Because even though motherhood doesn't come with any sort of primer, we know that it's our job to protect and help guide our kids, not judge their shitty taste in music since some of us were just spoiled from the boy bands of the 90s and are now jaded souls.

I'll take all the eye rolls if it means I get to love her and watch her do life for as long as I'm here to see it. And I'll pass on the same advice to her that my mother gave me around her age and still does today.

It's unconventional and certainly not your typical "mom" advice, but the women in my family are far from typical. In my teen years and even now in my 40s, every single time I start an endeavor of any kind, my mother pays homage to a Miami classic song with so much bass I'm sure it breaks a sound barrier somewhere and makes every ass shake within a ten-mile radius as she says to me, "Shake what your mama gave ya!" And she means it. That's her way of urging me to give it my all. To pour myself into whatever I am doing and make my mark. So I'll pass that torch to my own tween. With every single thing she faces or sets out to accomplish, from TikTok and beyond, I will proudly say, "SHAKE WHAT YOUR MAMA GAVE YA!" and hope she listens.

RACHEL SOBEL—THE heart and mind behind the blog *Whineandcheezits*—is a South Florida native living the NEW normal: marriage, baby, divorce, remarriage, another baby.

In addition to writing her own blog, she's a contributor for *PopSugar*, *Mommy Nearest* and has work in *Scary Mommy*, *Romper*, *Huffington Post* and Today Show Parents. She's a speaker and a published author with essays in two anthologies about motherhood and pregnancy. Rachel also hosts a live show on Facebook and Instagram (@whineandcheezits)

every Monday night at 8:30 p.m.—from her closet, because THAT'S THE ONLY PLACE SHE CAN HIDE FROM HER CHILDREN!

After working many years in public relations and communications, she stopped with the "what ifs" and hatched a plan to leave the confines of a cubicle and live her dream as a full-time writer. (In her dream she was thinner, richer, and had much more clothing without spatterings of spit-up and breastmilk, but beggars can't be choosers.)

25

THE LAST TIME

BY ALEXANDRA ROSAS

The first book I read to him was a thick-paged cardboard illustrated wonder. The pages were made up of sturdy white images against glossy black. Just outlines of things he didn't yet recognize, but the shimmer of the pages held him. He was just a few days old then and didn't understand what I was saying and didn't yet identify what he was seeing, but we were reading together.

With his fluffy head against my full nursing breast, I would point and whisper into his dandelion wisps of hair. "That's a dog. See? Now here's a cat, sometimes they get along with each other. Sometimes they fight. Here's a ball, we'll play with that one day. Oh, and an apple. They are loud, and kind of sour! People bake them into pies." His favorite page one day became the one with the white bunny. When I would turn to it and the long, tall ears began to appear, he would slap his pudgy, double-dented baby fingers and squeal. It was the bunny!

White amidst black, and he loved it. The starkness against the shiny pitch kept his gaze. We first shared it on the night he was born. I had brought it with me to the hospital, packing it in my overnight bag because I had dreamed my whole life of one day having my own baby to read to, and finally, he was here. That night, that first time, I was just shy of 36 years old and had waited a lifetime to be reading to someone like this. I read to only him for fifteen months, holding him close. And then, his beautiful brother was born.

While my first would let me know the books he liked best with a joyful clap, it was the second born who was the one to sigh, content and happy, with anything, as long as he was with us. Then, there soon came a time when I was reading to three children. We began with this same black and white book, always their first book. Together, we fit on our bed, one boy across the top and two held under each of my arms. I laugh remembering how my husband waited across the bottom, but always falling asleep before we would finish. For every night of their young lives since we first brought them home, we read them to sleep, again, always beginning with our black and white cardboard book.

We moved on to other books as they grew older. Some of our chapter books taking just short of a month to finish, reading a chapter a night. *The Boxcar Children* series was a favorite, later it would spark my first son's interest in history. We would make our reading choices, finding delights at bookstores, rummage sales, libraries, mail-order catalogues, school book fairs. If there were books for sale, they would rush in to pick one for the nights ahead.

"Can we just get books that are only looking ones, Mom?"

"Yup, that's fine. It's good to take a break and just look," I would answer.

"How about anything that is some words but more pictures?"

"I think that's a good mix, don't you?"

And off they would go, happy excited voices, calling out the nights ahead for each of their choices. A history book for Monday, one on airplanes to start the weekend, other times sharing the same one together. Reading at night was what we did, and there was never a feeling of resistance or hesitance. We read at night. That's what the boys and I did.

We loved our books, but I'll tell you, the biggest shock we ever came against was, surprisingly, with *The Wizard of Oz*. We had all seen the movie one weekend night and I thought we all, including me, would have fun reading the original that the film was based on. After all, how different could it be, right? When we picked up the book from the library, it was a hefty load. But surely we had the determination and resilience to make it through. Well, try it sometime because you will be astonished at how unlike Frank Baum's original writing is from anything put out by MGM. We tried, but by our fourth night's reading, we found ourselves wishing for a tornado to come into our room and take Mr. Baum's book along with it.

The point is, I have always read to my children. It was how we ended our nights. With me and them, all of us in makeshift pajamas, never a matching top or bottom, and me falling into bed at the end of our day, hoping I'd stay up and be able to sneak back downstairs to finish the last household chores of the day. My three boys would cushion themselves around me—one wrapping himself around the top of my head, the other two, whose heads fit custom-made into my chest—and we would all fall into deep sighs and commence to read.

It was our life, and a guaranteed way to get them up to bed with never, ever a fight.

The stories we read were part of our night: first a snack, then a warm bath, pajamas, tooth-brushing, and all of us hopping under the blankets. Pillows piled up and all around, and together the four of us headed for a good night story.

It must have happened one night when my oldest son was in the seventh grade. He just went straight up to bed. Walking upstairs, he shouted back to us, "'Night, Mom, 'night, Dad. I'm going to bed now."

"Sleep good, baby," I shouted back, perplexed, but thinking he was just that tired. He had started after school basketball and had a science paper to be finished. But then, again, the next few nights, the same pattern of straight up to bed.

"Going up to bed now, Mom! Dad!"

I didn't want to pry, pre-adolescence is a delicate balance, so I called back the rest of the week, too. "Sleep tight, my baby. See you tomorrow, honey."

But the truth was that after that first night, I was now down to just two small bodies around me for a story at night. But then not much after that, the middle one told me that he wanted to go up with his older brother now, too. Would that be all right, he wanted to know.

"Of course, yes, you can both go up together, yes." I answered. "I love you, I'll see you tomorrow."

I was left with one together with me in bed, but even I know that children have to grow up. So, it was me with my youngest.

"Hey," I asked him when he was leaning in under my arm one night at bedtime. "How do you feel about keeping on reading our stories, us, without your brothers?"

"I like it, Mom. I was kind of feeling they were too old, too. But I like the stories."

I sighed, "Do you think I should ask them why, honey?" The truth is, I really did want to know.

"No. I think they'll feel guilty about saying anything. When it's your mom, you always feel like she'll cry about everything."

I laughed. They knew me so well. Yes, everything about them growing up did make my eyes sting with tears. I laughed because the truth is funny, and the truth does hurt. I would in fact probably cry if I asked them about going to bed without stories anymore.

The older ones knew when it was time to be finished with that part of our life together.

The youngest one knew just where he still wanted to be.

For a while, anyway.

And tonight, right now on this night, it's just me. I read my own book at night to myself. I don't read to anyone anymore.

I'm here, under a blanket, my two pillows behind me.

And I can't help but wish that I would have known that the last time I read to my children, I would have known it was, the last time.

ALEXANDRA ROSAS IS a first-generation American who has been writing cultural memoir and humor since 2006. She was Co-Producer of the nationally acclaimed *Listen To Your Mother* Show and is multiple winner of the BlogHer Voice of The Year Award. Alexandra has been featured on The Moth Radio Hour and is a Grand Slam Moth Stage winner. Her writing has been published on various sites including *Scary Mommy*, BlogHer, Purple Clover, and *Huffington Post Latino Voices*. She was awarded the National Gold and Silver Parenting Media Award two years in a row for her MetroParent syndicated column on parenting teens, "MomLogic."

26

THE KIDS ARE ALL RIGHT

BY JEN MANN

We arrived bright and early for our first day at Universal Studios Orlando. The gates hadn't opened yet, but it was already getting crowded. It was a school holiday, so we were surrounded by large groups of barely supervised teenagers from all over the world. They wore brightly colored t-shirts proclaiming their group affiliations. There were high school marching bands, cheerleading squads, dance teams, and more. The girls were taking a ridiculous number of selfies and the boys were rough housing. The squeals of excitement and bursts of laughter hurt my brain and my ears. As I was jostled by a group of teens for the hundredth time, I felt my middle-aged patience wearing thin. I barely had patience for my own children, whom I loved; I definitely had none for a bunch of stranger's kids.

A boy stepped on my foot. He tossed an apology over his shoulder. "Sorry, ma'am."

A girl flipped her ponytail in my eye. "Oops," she muttered.

The rage started to build. I'm raising two teenagers so I know first-hand what sort of assholes kids can be. They are selfish and self-centered. They are rude and gross. They make poor decisions and act like dummies. And for some reason, I'd decided to spend the next four days surrounded by thousands of them. "This was a terrible mistake," I muttered. "Teenagers suck."

"Come on, Mom," Adolpha grabbed my hand. "The gates are opening. Let's catch the train to Hogsmeade."

We surged forward with the crowd and I felt my rage ebb because Butterbeer always makes me feel better. We picked up our pace and headed toward the ride. That's when I saw the girl in front of me. She was in a teal t-shirt and a white skirt. My initial thought was, *Damn, youngling, must be nice to have enough thigh gap to be able to wear a skirt in Orlando humidity without fear of chub rub. I'd have a rash just getting from the parking lot to the front gate.* I was still mourning my youth when I saw she had a large dark red splotch on the back of her skirt.

"Oh no," I whispered to Adolpha. "That girl got her period."

Adolpha nodded solemnly. "Oh, that sucks for her."

"What should we do?" I asked.

"I don't know," Adolpha said. "I don't have any supplies with me. And her skirt's already ruined. She needs new clothes."

I had a momentary flashback to the many times in my life where I'd seen girls and women with blood stains on their pants along with the couple times those were my ruined pants. I could already hear the mean-spirited taunts from the girls and the gross commentary from the boys. I couldn't let her walk around like that all day with people snickering and talking behind her back. But what could I do? I didn't have anything with me. I could go into a gift shop and buy her some shorts, but would that be weird? She was walking with a boy and they were flirting with one another and I couldn't imagine interrupting them and being like, "Hi, you don't know me, but could I buy you some tampons and a pair of souvenir shorts? Are you a Gryffindor or a Slytherin?"

Totes awk, as the kids would say.

But what if Adolpha was at the park with a group of kids and she bled through her shorts? What would I want someone to do? I would want someone to help her. "Screw it. I'm going in," I said. The crowd swelled and I lost sight of the girl in the teal shirt for a minute, but then I caught a glimpse of her. She was only about ten feet in front of us. I just needed to pick up my pace and I could be to her in a few seconds. The morning was cool, so I was wearing a sweatshirt. I pulled it over my head as I sped up, prepared to tie it around her waist.

Just before I reached her, I saw a swarm of bright green out of the corner of my eye. It was a group of about five girls, all in matching bright green t-shirts making a beeline for the teal shirt girl. They were going to beat me to her. My stomach tensed up and I felt sick. I was positive the green shirt group was going to do something malicious to the teal shirt girl. Why did I think that? Because I'm an asshole who projects all my shit onto other people. When I was a teenager, girls would have pounced like a pack of lions on a weak gazelle. They could literally smell the blood soaking through your white shorts. I was positive this was going to end badly for the girl in teal and I felt compelled to intervene. All morning long I'd been dealing with rowdy, inconsiderate teens and I was positive this group was no different. I tried to speed up but the green shirts beat me handily.

I watched as the green girl gang quickly engulfed the teal shirt girl. They formed a tight circle around her, cutting her off from the boy she'd been walking with. My jaw dropped as I realized they'd formed a circle around her not to attack her, but to protect her. While one girl told the boy, "Sorry, she'll be right back. We have something she needs," another girl whispered frantically into her ear. I could tell by the way the girl in the teal shirt tensed up, she'd been told she'd been walking around for who knows how long with a bright red spot on her butt. I saw her shoulders slump with embarrassment. But the green gang wasn't having any of that. "It's okay," a third girl said, reaching into her backpack and pulling out a pair of shorts. "I've got you covered."

By now I was practically stopped and watching the whole scenario play out. The circle never broke as they sliced through the crowd toward the nearest ladies' room, the girls working together in a pack. But not like a pack of wolves, but more like a pack of future mama bears. A pack of young women who understood the power of women supporting women. A pack of young women who knew it was better to lift up one another rather than tear each other down.

I slung an arm around Adolpha's shoulders and pulled her in for a hug, despite her protests. "Mom!"

"Oh, shush," I said. "I was wrong. Teenagers don't suck at all. Let's go catch the train!"

JEN MANN IS BEST KNOWN for her wildly popular and hysterical blog *People I Want to Punch in the Throat*. She has been described by many as Erma Bombeck—with f-bombs. Jen is known for her hilarious rants and funny observations on everything from parenting to gift giving to celebrity behavior to politics to Elves on Shelves. She does not suffer fools lightly. Jen is the author of the *New York Times* bestseller *People I Want to Punch in the Throat: Competitive Crafters, Drop-Off Despots, and Other Suburban Scourges* which was a Finalist for a Goodreads Reader's Choice Award. Her latest book is *How I F*cking Did It: From Moving Elves to Making Over Six-Figures on the Internet and You Can Too*. She is also the mastermind behind the *New York Times* bestselling *I Just Want to Pee Alone* series. Jen is an author, publisher, speaker, award-winning blogger, podcaster, and social media influencer with over 1 million fans across all her platforms.

JEN IS a married mother of two children who she calls Gomer and Adolpha in her writings—she swears their real names are actually worse.

NOTES FROM THE EDITOR

Thank you for reading our stories. We all appreciate your support and we hope you enjoyed it. We also hope you will tell a friend—or thirty about this. If you liked the book please do us a huge favor and leave us a review. Of course, we prefer 5-star, but we'll take what we can get.

If you enjoyed this book then you'll love following all of us on social media!

OTHER BOOKS AVAILABLE

I Just Want to Pee Alone **Anthology Series**

I Just Want to Pee Alone

I STILL Just Want to Pee Alone

I Just Want to Be Alone

I Just Want to Be Perfect

But Did You Die?

You Do You!

Will Work for Apples

People I Want to Punch in the Throat **Series**

People I Want to Punch in the Throat: Competitive Crafters, Drop Off Despots, and Other Suburban Scourges

Spending the Holidays with People I Want to Punch in the Throat: Yuletide Yahoos, Ho-Ho-Humblebraggers, and Other Seasonal Scourges

Working with People I Want to Punch in the Throat: Cantankerous Clients, Micromanaging Minions, and Other Supercilious Scourges

Just a Few People I Want to Punch in the Throat (Vols. 1-6 compilation)

Also by Jen Mann

How I F*cking Did It: From Moving Elves to Making Over Six-Figures on the Internet and You Can Too

My Lame Life: Queen of the Misfits

Made in the USA
Middletown, DE
26 August 2020